# STOCK MARKET INVESTING FOR BEGINNERS 2021

STOCK MARKET INVESTING FOR BEGINNERS 2020: A GUIDE TO START INVESTING IN THE STOCK MARKET, LEARN THE BASICS, HOW TO BUY YOUR FIRST STOCK AND MAKE YOUR MONEY GROW. THE ULTIMATE GUIDE TO GET STARTED

## MORGAN RICH

**Copyright - 2020 -**

**All rights reserved.**

The content contained within this book may not be reproduced, duplicated or transmitted without direct written permission from the author or the publisher.

Under no circumstances will any blame or legal responsibility be held against the publisher, or author, for any damages, reparation, or monetary loss due to the information contained within this book. Either directly or indirectly.

**Legal Notice:**

This book is copyright protected. This book is only for personal use. You cannot amend, distribute, sell, use, quote or paraphrase any part, or the content within this book, without the consent of the author or publisher.

**Disclaimer Notice:**

Please note the information contained within this document is for educational and entertainment purposes only. All effort has been executed to present accurate, up to date, and reliable, complete information. No warranties of any kind are declared or implied. Readers acknowledge that the author is not engaging in the rendering of legal, financial, medical or professional advice. The content within this book has been derived from various sources. Please consult a licensed professional before attempting any techniques outlined in this book.

By reading this document, the reader agrees that under no circumstances is the author responsible for any losses, direct or indirect, which are incurred as a result of the use of information contained within this document, including, but not limited to, - errors, omissions, or inaccuracies.

# TABLE OF CONTENTS

**INTRODUCTION** — 5

**CHAPTER 1**
Introduction to Stock Market — 9

**CHAPTER 2**
Basics of Stock market — 19

**CHAPTER 3**
How to Buy Your First Stock — 55

**CHAPTER 4**
Basic Strategies in the Stock Market — 69

**CHAPTER 5**
Analyzing Stock Markets — 79

**CHAPTER 6**
Advanced analysis to pick right stocks — 97

**CHAPTER 7**
Risks in Stock Market — 121

**CONCLUSION** — 139

# INTRODUCTION

Congratulations on downloading Stock Market Investing for Beginners and thank you for doing so.

The following chapters will discuss about stock marketing in detail with beginners in mind. We will also discuss different technical analysis methods that will help us understand how stock markets work and principles we need to adapt to succeed in markets. It is a known fact that stock markets are random and predicting is just a mere myth. But understand the fact that randomness can be analyzed if we have a lot of known parameters. That easily defines if you have a lot of real-time knowledge about all the related things that are going on with the stock you bought you will easily know whether to hold it or not. We will discuss a lot of these topics in our book in detail.

For the investors who are preparing to invest in the stock market, the basic method of learning how to open an account, watch the market, and mastering the computer and mobile phone stock apps is an extremely important compulsory course. The correct stock trading skills can improve the accuracy of the stock price trend forecast, thus directly affecting the success or failure of an investor's investment.

To this end, through continuous summarization and practice we have compiled this book. From the practical point of view, this book will have the necessary knowledge of watching the market. The organic combination of the actual application skills of the stocks that need to be mastered enables the investors to apply them to the actual stock market investment and gain income after learning the relevant methods.

This book carefully selects the most practical methods and techniques in stock investment to focus on the first step, first the entry knowledge, then the four actual combat, then the six major analysis, and finally a new level, in the description process that is easy-to-understand way to describe and explain the entire knowledge structure.

There are countless techniques and methods for stock investment. The techniques and methods listed in this book are comprehensive. Shareholders do not need to master all of them. They can select several technologies to study in depth and summarize them in a comprehensive way and achieve good investment results. Readers should also flexibly adapt to the actual situation in reading, and make a good habit of diligent thinking and form a good inductive summarizing ability.

This book is for:

1. Just getting started and investors who want to further improve their stock trading skills.

2. Investors who want to improve their steady profitability through the bullish market management skills.

3. Online stock trading materials for colleges and universities or enterprises.

4. Reader as a training company for the training, guidance and communication of securities companies and fund companies.

You will however need to concentrate well in understanding the concepts that we explain here. Before starting remember that failure and loss is a normal thing in investing. Never give up and don't lose hope.

There are plenty of books on this subject on the market, thanks again for choosing this one! Every effort was made to ensure it is full of as much useful information as possible, please enjoy!

# CHAPTER 1

# Introduction to Stock Market

If people are stumbled with a simple question " What is the biggest investment market?" almost every one of them will say that is stock market. It was obvious and the craze for stock market investing has touched many people all over the world. It is also one of the most famous investing sources for people who work and have an idea of saving some money for the future. To understand stock and stock markets in a perfect manner one need to start appreciating wealth and how it runs the world.

As the saying goes from the records, "The stock is calculated from the perspective of investment." Stocks can be described as the most popular investment method. Before learning to invest in stocks, investors must understand the relevant knowledge of stocks, clarify the concept and types of stocks, and understand the stock market and stock prices. It is also better if one knows Knowledge of the index and factors affecting stock prices.

## What Is Stock?

So, why does stocks have such a high rate of return, and what exactly is it?

A stock is a kind of securities. The stock we usually refer to refers to common stock, which is a share of ordinary rights in the company's management and that closely deals with the profit and distribution of property. Conceptually, stocks are stock certificates issued by a company limited by shares to investors when raising capital, representing the ownership of the company by its holders (i.e. shareholders).

For example, suppose a joint stock company has 100 shareholders, each of whom contributes 100,000 dollars, each of whom owns 1% of the company's ownership (equity). After the company has been approved by the competent authority, the stock is printed and handed over to the investor as a certificate of ownership. This is the original meaning of the stock.

Stocks can generally be transferred by way of sale and purchase. Shareholders can recover their investment through stock transfer, but they cannot ask the company to return their capital. Shareholders can buy and sell these stocks in the stock market, which constitutes the circulation of stocks in the hands of different investors and changes in ownership and holdings.

Stocks, like ordinary goods, have prices, can be bought and sold, and can be used as collateral. Anyone who owns these stocks can become a shareholder of the company. The relationship between shareholders and the company is not a creditor-debtor relationship. The shareholder is the owner of the company where the company has limited liability, risk-taking and sharing of income to the extent of its capital contribution.

Therefore, stocks are securities issued by the stock company to investors to prove their shareholder rights and investment shares in the company and to obtain dividend income.

## Types of Stock

The stock is issued by the joint stock company to the shareholders and is the shareholder certificate of the shareholder investment. The stocks are classified according to a variety of methods. According to the classification of dividends, it can be divided into several types. According to the enjoyment of voting rights, it can be divided into three types: single right, multiple powers, and no power.

1. Single-weight stocks: A single-weight stock means the shareholder has only one voting right.

2. Multi-right stocks: Multi-equity stocks are stocks that give the shareholder multiple voting rights per stock.

3. Unauthorized stocks: Unauthorized stocks are

stocks that do not have voting rights.

In addition to classifying stocks according to the principle of classification, we often hear words such as "A shares" and "B shares" in daily life, which is actually classified according to the way stocks are issued.

## Stock Listing Conditions

1. Stock listing refers to the legal act of publicly listing trading on the exchange after the stocks that have been issued have been approved by the stock exchange. The stock is listed as a "bridge" connecting stock issuance and stock trading.

2. The conditions for the termination of listing of shares are as follows.

3. The listed company's total share capital and shareholding distribution have changed, and no longer have listing conditions. The listing conditions cannot be met within the time limit set by the stock exchange.

4. The listed company does not disclose its financial accounting report in accordance with the regulations, or has False records of financial accounting reports and has refused to correct them.

5. The listed company has suffered consecutive losses for three years and failed to resume profitability in the following year.

6. The listed company is dissolved or declared bankrupt.

## Ways of Issuing Shares

Before the stock is issued, the listed company signs an agency issuance contract with the agent issuing securities firm of the stock, determines the way the stock is issued, and clarifies the responsibilities of the parties. The method of issuing stock agents is different according to the risks assumed by the issuance. It is generally divided into two types: underwriting and issuance.

Through the underwriting method of stock listing, although listed companies can raise a large amount of funds in the short term, they can cope with the urgent need for funds. However, securities that are generally underwritten, securities underwriters are only purchased at the primary issue price of the stock or at a lower price, which inevitably causes the listed company to lose some of its due income.

In recent years the stock market has become one of the sole advantages for people who are trying to achieve financial management be investing in different sectors. For wannabe traders and investors, it is very important to acquire basic knowledge on how the stocks work. As a guide for beginners this book will introduce a lot of basic topics in detail for investors that are interested to start stock investing. Let us dive into the trading world.

## What Is a Stock Index?

The stock price index is compiled using the index method in statistics and is an indicator reflecting the overall price of the stock market or the movement and trend of certain stock prices.

The stock price index, also known as the stock price index, is a relative indicator that dynamically reflects the total price level of a stock market in a certain period. Specifically, the total price level of a certain base period is considered as 100. A relative number obtained by comparing the total price levels of stocks in each period, that is, the stock price index of each period can be known by this process. The stock price index is generally expressed as a percentage and is famously referred as "dot".

In essence, the stock index is the stock price average, but when calculating the stock index, the stock index and the stock price average are usually calculated separately. As a fact that the average stock price is expressed in arithmetic mean, it reflects the general level of price movements of multiple stocks.

The stock index is a relative indicator that reflects the stock price changes in different periods. This is the reason for which in a long period of time, the stock index can more accurately reflect the stock price changes and trends than the stock price average. The calculation of the stock price index has two methods: arithmetic average method and weighted average method.

However, in practice listed companies often increase, split, and pay dividends so that stock prices have the effect of ex-rights and ex-dividends which makes them losing continuity and makes them impossible to be directly compared. Therefore, in the calculation of the stock price index, we must also take into account the changes in these factors, and correct the index in time to avoid distortion of the stock price index.

## Stock Exchange Market

There are many stock markets exchanges all around the world. One need to understand in depth to invest in stock markets. Sufficient and moderate knowledge is an essential prerequisite before starting any investment because many factors are responsible for the fluctuation of stock prices. We will in detail discuss below the famous stock exchanges in the world.

### 1. New York Stock Market

The New York Stock Exchange is an important part of the New York capital market. In the United States, more than 10 stock exchanges are registered under the Securities Exchange Act and are listed as national exchanges. Among them, the New York Stock Exchange, NASDAQ and the American Stock Exchange are the largest, they are located in New York.

The New York Stock Exchange (NYSE) is located on Broadway Street and is arguably the nerve center of the world economy. The New York Stock Exchange is the first exchange of listed companies with the highest market capitalization, the number of IPOs and the market value, and the second trading volume. At the end of April 2005, NYSE acquired the all-electronic stock exchange (Archipelago) and became a profitable institution.

It is reported that there are about 2,800 companies listed on the New York stock market, with a global market capitalization of $15 trillion. In the course of more than two hundred years of development New York Stock Exchange has expanded its name and prestige hundreds of times.

The Institute has played a pivotal role in the development of the US economy, the smooth progress of socialized production, and the construction of a modern market economic system.

2. Tokyo Stock Market

The Tokyo Stock Exchange is one of Japan's stock exchanges, referred to as "Dongzhen", headquartered in Tokyo. Although the history of the development of the Tokyo Stock Exchange is not long when compared in NYSE it is one of the largest securities trading centers in the world and the second-largest securities market in the world after the New York Stock Exchange.

The Tokyo Stock Exchange, along with the Osaka Stock Exchange and the Nagoya Stock Exchange, are among the top three stock exchanges in Japan, and their market size ranks among the top three in the world and is also Japan's most important economic center. At present, there are 1,777 listed companies in the Tokyo Stock Exchange, including 110 foreign companies, with a total market capitalization of nearly $4.5 trillion.

3. London Stock Market

The London Stock Exchange (LSE) is one of the world's four largest stock exchanges. As the world's most international financial center, London is not only the global leader in European bond and foreign exchange trading.

First, it also accepts more than two-thirds of the international equity underwriting business.

As the world's third-largest securities trading center, the London Stock Exchange is the world's oldest stock exchange. The London Stock Exchange plays a central role in operating the world's strongest stock market, with foreign stocks trading more than any other stock exchange.

4. Chinese Stock Market

The Shanghai Stock Exchange, the Shenzhen Stock Exchange, the Hong Kong Stock Exchange, and the Taiwan Stock Exchange comprise the large Chinese stock market. The most important of these is the

Shanghai Stock Exchange, which was established on November 26, 1990 and opened on December 19 of the same year.

In the next chapter, we will have a brief look at the basics of stock marketing in detail.

# CHAPTER 2

# Basics of Stock Market

In this chapter we will start with an explanation of New York stock index which we will take as a reference in this book. However, every stock index or market around the world follow same methodology. Let us start!

## What Is the New York Composite Index?

The NYE Stock Index is a stock index compiled by the New York Stock Exchange and officially released on December 19, 1890. The sample of the stock index is all stocks listed on the New York Stock Exchange. The newly listed stocks will be included in the calculation of the stock index on the second day of listing.

Since the New York Stock Exchange Index is calculated based on the total share capital of each listed company, the large stocks can influence the trend of the New York Composite Index, such as

Google and Amazon. The release of the stock index is almost synchronous with the changes in the stock market. It is an important reference for investors and securities practitioners to study and judge the trend of stock price changes.

The relationship between the two indicator lines of the SSE stock index is applied as follows.

### 1) When the New York Composite Index rises

When the yellow line trended above the white line, it indicated that the small stocks rose more. When the yellow line trend is below the white line trend, it indicates that the small stocks have a smaller increase than the large stocks with large weights.

### 2) When the New York Composite Index falls

When the yellow line trended above the white line, it indicated that the small stocks fell less than the larger and stronger stocks. When the yellow line trended under the white line trend, it indicated that the small stocks fell more than the large and powerful stocks.

## What is the New York Stock Index?

The New York Composite Stock Index is a stock index compiled by the New York Stock Exchange. The calculation method of the stock index is basically the same as that of the Stock Exchange. The sample is all the stocks listed on the New York Stock Exchange, and the weight is the total number of shares of the stock.

At present, the New York Stock Exchange has two stock indices: one is the old index that is New York Composite Index, and the other is the current constituent stock index. The difference between the two indices is not large.

New York Stock Exchange (or New York Component Index) is a stock index of New York Stock Exchange. It is one of the most well-known indexes in USA's securities market.

A sample of 40 listed companies with market representation in the selected Stock Exchanges was sampled and is using the tradable share capital as the weight, calculated by the weighted average method. Market representation, liquidity and blue-chip characteristics are defined to be followed by these exchanges.

## Recognize the Division of Stocks

At present, there are as many as 2,800 listed companies. The board and the stock exchange will classify them and classify them according to industry.

There are five main reasons for the division of stocks that is region, industry, performance, equity size, and concept. However, the criteria for the division of the sector are not static, and a listed company can belong to multiple different sectors at the same time, thus having multiple identities.

For investors, the industry division can clearly know the main business of a listed company, for when it chooses stocks and investment fields. The important help is an important basis for making a preliminary judgment – whether to buy a stock, especially for fundamental investors.

For example, Tesla belongs to the section according to the location of the company. It belongs to the transportation section according to the industry of the company. It belongs to the middle stocks according to the size of the share capital (80 million shares of circulation), and belongs to the concept of the Olympics. However, when the above-mentioned various sectors have a linkage market, Tesla may also have linkages.

### What Is an ST stock?

ST stocks are a very common stock in the stock market. When we enter the stock market, we will find that this stock is very conspicuous because of various reasons that are mandatory such as stock price. In addition to the contrary beliefs some parameters are also prefixed with an asterisk so that we are new to the market. There must be doubts at the time when we start investing but they will slowly fade out as we acquire knowledge in the expertise.

ST is an abbreviation for English which means "special treatment." The title ST is the listed company that has financial status or other abnormal conditions. In short, ST stocks are stocks that cause risk warnings due to certain events. The ST prefix is actually a risk warning. Generally, ST stocks are added because of financial and illegal operations.

ST stocks are limited to 5%. It should be pointed out that "special treatment" is not a punishment for listed companies, but an objective reminder of the current situation of listed companies. The purpose is to alert investors to market risks and guide investors to make rational investments. The company's abnormal situation is eliminated, and normal transactions can be resumed, and the ST title can be canceled.

ST shares can be prefixed, and naturally, the bad name the share holds can be removed. The process of going to the ST prefix is generally called uncapping. ST stocks usually only need to eliminate the risk warning, and there is no other risk warning reason.

## What Is a Large-Cap Stock?

There is no uniform standard for large-cap shares. Generally, it is customary to refer to stocks with relatively large share capital. It is worth noting that the total share capital is more than several billion shares. The advantage of large-cap stocks is that they are highly resilient and the dealers are less likely to operate, making them the first choice for defensive or long-term value investments.

Stocks such as Apple, Microsoft, Amazon which have more than one billion or even billions of shares, are called super-cap stocks.

In terms of price-earnings ratio, stocks with the same performance, small-cap stocks have higher P/E ratios than mid-cap stocks, and mid-cap stocks are higher than large-cap stocks. Especially when the market is weak, there are more opportunities for small cap stocks. In the bull market, large-cap stocks and mid-cap stocks are more suitable for large funds to enter and exit, so the large stocks are more optimistic.

The influence is large and often becomes a tool for market regulation index. Investors choose individual stocks. Generally, the bear market should choose small-cap stocks and small-cap stocks. The bull market should choose large-cap stocks and medium-sized stocks.

The investment techniques of large-cap stocks are as follows.

1) Buying skills

Investing in large-cap stocks does not mean that all stocks are worth buying. Among them the form is very important as we must choose the stock price at the bottom and notice whether the increase is far less than the stock index. We also need to observe whether it has completed the bottom of the fund and is about to enter the rising stage of the stock.

## 2) Selling skills

When the stock price rises to a certain extent, and the various stock reviews have been recommended, this is the time to sell. In addition, in the process of rising large-cap stocks, there is rarely a continuous daily limit, and it is often the cumulative increase in a period of time that brings lucrative returns to investors. Therefore, holding large-cap stocks cannot have short return investments but steady investments of a period of time which is the biggest advantage of large-cap stocks.

## P/E ratio

Earnings ratio (P/E ratio), also known as the ratio of stock return or price-to-earnings ratio, is the ratio of stock market price to earnings per share. The formula is: price-earnings ratio = (current market price per share) ÷ (after tax per share) profit). At present, a P/E ratio indicator is printed on several large securities newspapers and magazines. This allows stock investors to monitor the daily stock market intelligence table.

If the purchase of stocks is purely for the purpose of obtaining dividends, and the company's performance has remained the same, then the dividend income has the same meaning as the interest income. For investors, whether to deposit money into the bank or buy stocks depends first and foremost on Whether he is enthusiastic about high return on investment. Therefore, when the stock price-earnings ratio is lower than the standard price-earnings ratio calculated by the bank interest rate and the funds will be used to purchase stocks. Otherwise, the funds will flow to the bank deposits. This is the simplest and most intuitive price-earnings ratio.

## P/B ratio

The P/B ratio refers to the ratio of stock price per share to net assets per share, and is also one of the important indicators in stock investment analysis. The P/B ratio is calculated as: P/B = (P÷BV), which is the price per share (P) / Book Value per share.

The net stock value mainly includes the total of the company's capital, capital reserve, capital public welfare fund, statutory reserve fund, discretionary reserve fund, undistributed surplus and other items. It represents the common interest enjoyed by all shareholders, also known as net assets. The amount of net assets is determined by the operation status of the joint-stock company. The better the operating performance of the company, the faster its asset appreciation. It is also important to know that the higher the net value of the stock more the shareholders rights on the stock.

For investors, according to the P/B selection criteria, the lower the P/B ratio, the lower the risk factor. However, when judging the value of the investment, we must also consider the market environment at the time, as well as the company's operating conditions and profitability. Especially in the bear market, the P/B ratio has become one of the preferred stock-picking indicators for investors. The reason is that the P/B ratio can reflect the safety margin of the stock price.

## Increase

The increase refers to the current increase in the stock. The formula for calculating the increase is: the increase = (current price - the closing price of the previous trading day), the closing price of the previous trading day × 100%.

## Amplitude

The stock amplitude is the percentage of the difference between the highest and lowest prices on the day after the stock opens, and the percentage of the previous day's closing price. It shows the stock's activity to a certain extent.

Data analysis of stock amplitudes is a great help for investigating stocks and is an indicator of market activity. The greater the amplitude of individual stocks, the deeper the involvement of the main funds, and vice versa. But it cannot be generalized, and it is necessary to analyze the specific stock price fluctuation range. If there is a relatively large market phenomenon in the relative historical low position, it means that the main funds are intervening. And on the contrary, the above phenomenon occurs at a relatively high historical level, which usually indicates that the main capital of the institution is fleeing.

## Multiparty and Empty Parties

Multi-party and empty parties are two common terms in the stock market.

In the stock market, or in other securities markets, there are long and short positions: the so-called long position means that investors are optimistic about the direction of the market, so they buy first, then sell, to earn profits. The other one is the difference called as the so-called short position means that investors or speculators see the trend of the future market decline, so they throw the securities in their hands and then wait for an opportunity to buy. Among them, the purchase is called a multi-party, and the short-selling is called an empty party.

Short selling also has the same day closing and continuous closing. Closing the day means closing the position on the day or the previous one (the explanation for "short selling" does not refer to the specific market. In theory, it can be closed on the same day, such as the Indian stock market implements the T+0 trading model, which can be bought and sold on the same day. The continuous liquidation refers to the open positions that were bought on the same day or that existed before.

## Dividend

Dividend is the dividend paid by the company to investors in a certain proportion of the stock share each year when it makes a profit. It is the return on investment of the listed company to shareholders.

Investors buy shares in a listed company, invest in the company, and enjoy the company's right to dividends. Generally speaking, there are two main forms of dividends for listed companies that is the distribution of cash dividends and stock dividends to shareholders. Listed companies may choose one of the forms to distribute dividends according to the situation, or they may use both forms simultaneously.

1. Cash dividend: refers to the payment of dividends to shareholders in cash, which is called dividends or dividends.

2. Stock dividends: refers to the fact that listed companies distribute stocks to shareholders. Dividends appear in the form of stocks, also known as bonus shares or share offerings.

3. Transfer of share capital: Investors often encounter cases in which listed companies transfer share capital. The transfer of share capital means that the company converts the capital reserve into share capital. The transfer of share capital does not change the shareholders' equity, but it increases the size of the share

capital, so the objective result is similar to the bonus share. In layman's terms, capital is used to transfer shares to shareholders.

The transfer of share capital and dividends is different. Dividends are undistributed profits. They are distributed to shareholders after deducting expenses such as provident fund. This is a way for shareholders to earn income. The transfer of share capital is a form of share offering by listed companies.

It is extracted from the provident fund, and the profits of the listed company over the years and the proceeds from the issuance of new shares at a premium are realized through the form of share offering. However, in practice, the effect of sending bonus shares and transferring share capital is roughly the same.

### Ex-dividend

When a listed company distributes stock dividends to shareholders, that is, when the company's surplus is converted into capital increase or stock placement, the stock price must be ex-divided and when the listed company distributes the surplus to shareholders in cash then the stock price will be ex-dividend. Shareholders who purchase shares of the company on the ex-dividend date may not enjoy the dividend distribution or allotment.

When a listed company announces a share offer or a rights issue, the stock is called a rights-bearing stock before the bonus share has been allocated and the rights issue has not yet been implemented. The company that wants to handle the ex-rights procedure must first report to the competent authority for approval. After granting the ex-rights, the company can determine the equity registration base date and the ex-rights benchmark date. Shareholders who own the stock on the share registration date are entitled to receive or subscribe for equity, and can participate in dividends or rights issues.

In fact, the purpose of ex-rights and ex-dividends is to adjust the value of each stock of the listed company so that investors can compare and analyze the stock price. If the ex-dividend and ex-dividend treatments are not carried out, the stock price of the listed company will show a large fluctuation.

## Getting Started: Opening a Stock Account

A stock account is an account opened by an investor at a brokerage firm for stock trading. As a new investor, before entering the stock market for securities trading, you must first open a stock account. With this "passport", you can trade securities. Opening a stock account is a prerequisite for investors to enter the stock market.

## Understanding the process of stock trading in the market

As the saying goes: "Do not arbitrarily buy stocks at random, you must do some homework before investing to be successful." After understanding the basic knowledge of stocks, investors must also specify how to conduct stock trading and specific matters needing attention. As well as various trading operations, etc., only when you are prepared, you can move forward steadily.

### Basic Process of Stock Trading

Investors who have small and medium level capital have few disadvantages like less knowledge on how the stock market and trading work for example. While starting it feels too overwhelming to spend time reading market theory and market. This usual disadvantage of less knowledge may be prone to a great risk when trading and investing in stocks.

Therefore, the stock market must first understand the various stocks in a comprehensive and detailed manner, understand the listed companies, master the stock market, look at the six roads, listen to the eight parties, and carefully trade. Among them, the most important point is to be familiar with the stock trading process.

The first thing a new investor has to do is to open a stock account (i.e. shareholder card) for themselves. A stock account is equivalent to a "bank account", and investors can only buy and sell securities if they open a stock account.

In short, success requires the right approach, and stock trading is a profound knowledge. If you think that you can make money by buying and selling stocks casually, and you rush into the market, you will lose a lot. We suggest that investors must keep in mind the trading process of stock trading and accumulate certain stock knowledge and operational experience in order to obtain investment success.

## Basic Process of Opening an Account

Opening an account is also known as opening an account, and investors can apply at the brokerage counter or online. There are many brokers in USA which can open an account for you. Just do a quick research in google about best brokers in your region. Investors can choose one which they like to open an account.

At present, if you want to buy and sell stocks listed in NYSE, investors need to open the New York Stock Exchange stock account respectively.

You can also join by using the company or its authorized account opening agent. For example, Google Securities Registration Co., Ltd. is the only statutory body for investors in New York.

## Choosing the Right Transaction Type

It is the investors' responsibility to choose their own trading methods, as well as access methods to use in the future. They need to sign the appropriate opening dealings with the securities business department that includes bank transfer, telephone entrustment, mobile phone stock trading, and online trading, to name some.

Nowadays, transactions are basically online transactions. Investors should consider whether there are online consultation services, stock mobile phone trading software, telephone voice report, and other services, in addition to online transactions so that the transaction is convenient and smooth.

## Choosing a Securities Company That Suits You

Many investors who have just come into contact with the stock market may have such doubts. It is important to research which securities company is feasible and good for your trading.

## What kind of securities the company should be chosen?

Choosing a securities company that suits you is still very important for a newcomer. After all, in the case of a fast pace of life in modern society, it is necessary to prepare for work before opening an account, and to avoid the trouble of switching customers in the future.

## Stock Selection Practice Based on Multiple Elements

When the market is booming, why do you actively choose stocks, but still do not make money?

When the market is in a downturn, how to accurately choose growth stocks and firmly hold them?

Investors can only continue to stabilize their profits if they choose the growth stock based on the correct factors. This section not only allows you to completely abandon the law of inertia but also teaches you to be an investor who always thinks independently.

As the saying goes: "No matter what A shares and B shares are, making money is the only good stock." How to choose a good stock is the most urgent thing investors want to know. The stock market is broad and fluctuating, and there is no fixed good stock. It is very important for different investors to find stocks that suit their investment style. Regardless of whether the broader market falls or rises, stock-picking is the most important thing. It is difficult for you to make money if you choose stocks that are bad.

Investors have surpluses, losses, and different levels of profit and loss. In fact, they are mainly caused by different stock-picking. The idea and method of stock selection are varied and varied, but the most suitable stock selection method for retail investors should be the K-line chart.

There are very few investors who succeed in choosing the best stock and enjoy the huge return of investment when they sell those stocks back. It is a known fact after hundreds of interviews with the famous investors that they look at K-line chart of different stocks at every point of their trading time.

In the process of selecting stocks, the first choice is the shape of the stock. It is usually selected from the daily chart of the stock, and sometimes it is also selected by the weekly chart. This is completely reflected in the investor's personal preferences, and there is no regulation.

In short, the K-line study of stock opening, washing, and pulling up, some principled things will never be outdated. For example, the amount of open positions can determine the breakthrough height whereas the moving average system determines the breakthrough time. The control intention of line is simple and undisturbed whereas the price fluctuations do not leave space for short-term customers, and the volume must not be scattered.

### Element 1: Stock Selection Based on Fundamentals

The stock price often changes according to the fluctuations of fundamental factors such as certain economic indicators, economic policies, global economic situation, and domestic and foreign emergencies. The analysis of these factors is the main basis for judging the current market conditions and selecting stocks.

Fundamentals include as described below in detail.

a) diplomacy and politics

b) finance and economics

c) exchange rates and interest rates

d) national conditions and popularity

e) social needs and market supply

f) economic cycles and stock market trends

g) regulatory agencies and listed companies

h) industry prospects and product mix, chairman and management

I) corporate growth and market share

j) debt ratio and profit margin

k) resource structure and market capacity.

It is no easy task to fully understand and be familiar with it. Only by learning while operating normally, while learning and operating, capital and knowledge and experience grow simultaneously.

Analysis of the market outlook:

We can understand a k-line chart of a company as explained below.

From the analysis of K-line chart, the company's performance is improving, and the future may continue to grow. The stock market is expected to continue to strengthen. As the country's economic situation continues to evolve and change, the country's economic policies will naturally make corresponding adjustments. The main impact of national economic policies on stock prices is always should be researched.

Therefore, investors must have a deep understanding of the country's major economic policies and conscientiously implement the entire stock trading process in order for investment to be successful. If investors can choose stocks according to policies, and at the same time spend time to understand the fundamentals of listed companies through market research, and then learn them to use technical analysis to select good buy points it will be easy to earn big money in the stock market.

In the period of inflation, if the price increase is too large, the actual assets of the residents will shrink, causing market instability. In order to control inflation, the state will push interest rates up, and liquidity in the market will decrease, thus causing stock prices to fall.

### Use of industry Development Prospects

When choosing stocks, we attach great importance to two conditions: First, the industry's development trend is good, and it can have a sustained upward trend in the foreseeable time. The Second reason is, it is easy to miss the bull stocks in the current period, so the industry turning point needs to be on the industry.

Use the development prospects of the industry to analyze the basic situation of the proposed investment company including the company's operation, management, financial status and future development prospects. The intrinsic value of the research company is used to determine the reasonable price of the company's stock.

And then by comparing the difference between the market price and the reasonable price one should determine whether to buy the company's stock. Usually when people choose stocks, they must consider the influence of industry factors and try to choose stocks in high-growth industries, and avoid choosing stocks in the sunset industry. For example, USA's communications industry is a typical sunrise industry. The listed companies in the communications category are favored in the stock market. Their market positioning is usually high, and they often become "high-priced aristocrats" in the stock market.

## Use Value Investment Stock Selection

The intrinsic value of a stock determines the price. To stabilize the profit and avoid the risk in time, the intrinsic value of the stock must be analyzed.

Value-for-money stock selection refers to the research of further sub-sectors in the industry with the best trend in the large sector. Followed by selecting the sub-sector with the strongest trend, and then selecting the fundamentals in the sub-industry according to the concept of value investment.

## Element 2: Selecting Stocks Based on Psychological Aspects

The stock-picking psychology is an activity in which investors make psychological expectations about the stock value when they choose the target. To Cultivate a good stock-picking psychology investor should pay attention to the following aspects:

First, take advantage of the trend and follow the bull market trend to select stocks, in order to get big profits or sometimes lose money.

second, make a portfolio investment by choosing different types of stocks. The target stocks are combined to invest in market opportunities and correct a bad stock-picking mentality.

### Prepare for stock selection

Some people say that the stock market is like a battlefield, and a battlefield without smoke can make investors become heroes of the world, and it can also make investors scared. For investors who want to enter the stock market, they must first be psychologically prepared.

## Using the stock price effect to select stocks

The Price Comparison effect refers to the direct comparison of the stock price in the secondary market with the direct comparison between the same type of company, such as operating results, tradable equity, and funds raised. Specifically, there are the following aspects.

a) For stocks between the same geographical sector, choose stocks with lower stock prices.

b) Compared with individual stocks in the same industry, choose stocks with lower stock prices.

c) Compared with the stocks of the same speculative stocks, choose stocks with lower stock prices.

d) For stocks of the same size as the tradable shares, choose stocks with lower stock prices.

The "price comparison effect" is one of the most important market drivers driving the ever-changing securities market. For example, the Tesla Electronics Group, which was listed in 2009, has a total initial share capital of 256 million dollars and a circulation of 70 million shares. The forecasted performance in 2009 was 0.17 dollar per share. The company is mainly engaged in the production of cars belonging to the Automobile industry from 2009.

Panasonic and other home appliance companies have fallen into the "dead aristocracy" in the market. Therefore, for such a company that is mainly based on home appliance production and has no future development prospects and poor business performance, investors generally adopt a scornful attitude. The stock price on the first day of listing showed a downward trend. The decline in the two days was nearly 30%.

However, market investors have also overlooked one of the most critical factors - the "price effect." In 2009, the stock price of home appliance stocks was still basically positioned at 10 dollar or more. At that time, Panasonic had a minimum of 12 dollar, Phillips had a minimum of 15 dollar, and Samsung had a minimum of 11 dollar. The average price reached more than 10 dollars, so the price of the Electronics Group, which was only 5 dollars at the time, was obviously undervalued. In the future, its share price would have doubled by 10 dollars in two months. The successful speculation of the stock can be said to be the best example of the opposite price effect.

## Bull Market and Bear Market Picking Skills

The stock market can change at any time. Investors should learn to buy stocks at different times, use the characteristics of each period, and comprehensively analyze and practice.

### 1. Bullish market

In the concept of rational investors, "it's not much of what you earn today in the stock market, but who is living in the stock market for a long time".

If you are thinking make more money than you are investing then there are too many cases of great joy and great sadness in the stock market. Many people who have been in the stock market a few years ago have already disappeared, and they fell before the bull market. Whoever survives for a long time means that the market gives more opportunities. New investors can pay attention to the "three highs" theory of short-term stock-picking.

## 2. Bearish market

In the bear market, the difficulty of stock-picking is far greater than the bull market, and the market is constantly going down. The decline, the trend of most stocks is also downgraded and only a very small number of stocks go against the trend. Although it is very difficult to select stocks in a bear market, there are certain ways to follow them, as follows.

- Select stocks whose fundamentals have undergone major changes and whose performance is expected to surge.

Whether in the bull market or in a bear market, such stocks are sought after. As the fundamentals have improved, they must be reflected in the stock market sooner or later. Of course, you need to pay attention to the timing when choosing, and don't wait until the stock price has risen to a high point.

- Select stocks with long-term good development

prospects.

A company with good development prospects is the target pursued by most people when they choose stocks. These companies have bright prospects for development, stable operations, and are favored by many people.

It may be high and the performance is measured in advance. However, in the bear market, it may fall sharply with the market, and even plummet, which provides investors with a good buying opportunity can get a good stock at a very low price. At the same time, it should be noted that the selection of such stocks should be based on the medium and long-term, and cannot be expected to obtain high profits in the short term.

- Select individual stocks involved by the main agency.

The main institutions in the stock market are powerful that the average small and medium-sized investors can compare with some inflexible weaknesses. Once they are involved in a single stock, they have to hold a long time, especially in a bear market unless they recognize the export bureau.

Otherwise, we must use every opportunity to rebound and wait for opportunities to raise stocks. Small and medium-sized retail investors should have a relatively large profit opportunity if they have the right time to intervene, the cost price is below the banker's level, and they should not be greedy for excessive profits.

- Select stocks that have fallen in the late bear market.

In the late bear market or the bear market has been going on for a long time, some stocks have fallen overall. By using comprehensive basic analysis and technical analysis the downside has been limited and can no longer fall. Even if the broader market continues to fall, these stocks will stop falling early and take the lead in rebounding.

The summary shows that the important thing in the bear market is to pay attention to the market trend and understand the hot spots in the market and the policy changes. Investors should choose not to buy instead, they should prepare for the future by preparing to select individual stocks, considering it would have a chance for bull market.

## Element 3: Stock-picking Based on Price Changes

Stock prices are highly unpredictable, and this is one of the reasons that stocks have higher returns. From the rise and fall of market stocks, you can find strong stocks and weak stocks on the disk. In general, the stock price is the leading indicator of market fundamentals that is, the stock price may have begun to react before the news has not reached the market. So, observing the fluctuations in stock prices helps to guess the actual changes in the market.

Therefore, stock investors must learn to understand market behavior and be a "smart lamb." Stock investors should not have individual fear effects and must have the strength to be the ruin of the boat by learning to choose stocks according to the market.

## Using market speculation to pick stocks

The subject matter is an excuse for speculating stocks and is a tool used to stimulate market sentiment. Some subjects do have substantive content, while others are purely rumors where some are even deliberately spread rumors. In addition, most of the subject matter of the listed company itself cannot be determined casually, and many specific situations require specific analysis. But the market is characterized by the fact that as long as there is subject matter, the market is willing to dig and accept, and the real role of the subject is neglected.

The theme of the stock market has both positive and negative effects. When using the theme to find the best investment opportunities and stock selection, the operation should pay attention to the problems.

For long-term value investment stock selection, it is generally necessary to choose stocks whose price is lower than the value, that is, the stock that usually costs 4 cents to buy one dollar. Any such stock must be a stock that is generally not favored by the market, so there will be low prices. The price is in the top shipping phase or at the bottom of the pull-up phase.

## Using market hotspot stock-picking

In a popular saying: Hotspots are the sectors or stocks that are popular in a given period of time. These stocks that are popular in a certain period of time are often referred to by investors as "hot stocks" at the time. If investors look at the stock's rise and fall, they will find that they are mostly in the forefront of the rise.

It should be noted that there is no constant hot spot in the stock market. Similarly, there are no constant strong stocks and weak stocks. As the saying goes, "the wind and water turn", the strong stocks and strong sectors in a certain period may become weak stocks and weak sectors in another period, and vice versa.

Therefore, investors should always keep their heads clear and be good at adjusting their investment strategies in time according to the changes in market strength, so as to seize the new hot spots in the market in time.

For small and medium-sized retail investors, they can choose the corresponding stocks close to the market hotspots. People use Hot stock-picking, trend timing, small profits into profits, and then evolve into a stable profit model.

## Use of shareholder changes in stock selection

Changes in shareholder status are also an important reference factor for investors to choose stocks. For example, the number of shareholders is the number of all shareholders of a single stock. The smaller the number of people, the more concentrated the chips. In a more general way, the main force has already sucked up the goods, so the stock price will rise. On the contrary, if the number of shareholders increase it means that the main force is being distributed, and many of the chips are picked up by the retail investors. The stock price will naturally come down, and the profit will naturally fall.

In general, the change in the number of shareholders tends to complete a cycle from "a large number of people ☐ gradually decreasing ☐ the lowest value (inflection point) ☐ gradually increasing ☐ a large number of people". In these four stages, investors are more profitable when they intervene in the second stage, especially in the middle and late stages of this stage, the probability of success is quite high.

Investors need to conduct a statistical analysis of the changes in the number of shareholders to better grasp the trend of the market and individual stocks. Pay special attention to the several points shown in during the specific analysis.

## Using K-line stock-picking

The K-line chart is the basic means of stock analysis, allowing investors to fully and thoroughly observe the real changes in the market. From the K-line chart, you can see the overall trend of the market, as well as understand the fluctuations of the daily stock market. It is the most popular stock technical analysis method.

In the big bull market, it is often seen that the varieties that are continuously pulled up are exceptionally outstanding in short-term performance, and the returns are considerable. In the near-term market, such stocks are constantly emerging, and the opportunities are worthy of attention. As shown, it is the trend of Amazon Group from May 2014 to the beginning of 2014. In general, these short-term opportunities are all chasing operations, so it is necessary to find a strong and continuous rising variety to ensure that the participating stocks have sufficient short-term profit opportunities, and this can be found from the K-line. trace.

The stock selection focuses on the timing of the stock-picking, which is subject to an important principle - not to bottom out on the way down (because I don't know when it is the bottom). Only stocks with the trend established are selected. Among the stocks with established trends, the stocks with the strongest trend and the best gains are found to operate.

From the K-line analysis, those stocks that continue to rise generally have two situations:

First, far from the historical high, the current price is far lower than the average market cost of the stock and the rising resistance is very small.

Second, the stock is in the record is high, and the technical consolidation is relatively full. The chips have been mastered by large funds, and they are quickly separated from the cost area after rushing.

The general rule of operation of the market is: If a stock hits a new high (or recent high), then the probability of a new high in the future will be high; on the contrary, if a stock hits a new low (or recent low), then the possibility of a new low in a period of time is also great. Investors need to remember that stocks in the downtrend channel will only make you lose money or lose profit.

### Using the moving average stock-picking

The Moving Average (MA) originally means the moving average that is indeed calculated using different prerequisites. Since we make it into a line, it is generally called the moving average, or the moving average. It is the sum of the closing prices of a certain period of time.

The moving average line has indicators of 5 days, 10 days, 30 days, 60 days, 120 days, and 240 days. Among them, the 5-day and 10-day short-term moving averages are the reference indicators for short-term operations, called the daily average index; 30-day and 60-day are the medium-term moving average indicators, called the average moving average indicator; 120 days, 240 days is The long-term moving average indicator is called the annual average indicator.

Investors can use the moving average as a reference when selecting stocks.

Indicators that are present in the moving average can reflect the trend of the price trend. The so-called moving average is to average the stock price for a certain period of time, and then make an average line image based on this average. Investors can analyze the daily K-line chart and the average line in the same picture, which is very straightforward.

The most common method of moving averages is to compare the relationship between the moving average of the securities price and the price of the securities themselves. When the price of the security rises above its moving average, a purchase signal is generated. When the price of a security falls below its moving average, a sell signal is generated.

This signal is generated because it is believed that the "line" in the moving average is a strong criterion for supporting or blocking prices. Prices should rebound from the moving average. If it does not rebound and breaks through, then it should continue to develop in that direction until it finds a new level that can be maintained.

## Using morphological analysis to select stocks

Morphological analysis is a relatively concise and practical analysis method in the field of technical analysis. It summarizes and classifies some typical forms of stock price movements. Morphological analysis is a combination of a few days of K-line expansion to a period of tens of days or even a period. These numerous K-lines constitute a number of different trajectory patterns, and the long and short sides are analyzed by studying the trajectories that the stock price has passed. The contrast of power changes will make corresponding judgments to guide the actual operation.

## Using trend line stock-picking

The trend line is a graphical way to display the predicted trend of the data and can be used for predictive analysis which is also known as regression analysis. Use the trend line to extend the trend line in the chart to predict future data based on actual data.

An important principle of stock trading is that it is "following the trend" and cannot "move against the trend." Among them, "potential" is the direction and trend that is, the direction of stock price movement. Usually, there are three directions for the trend: an upward trend, a downward trend, and a horizontal trend (no trend).

In the stock market, investors can only make money by buying low and selling high, so it is especially important to select stocks with an upward trend. That is to say, in the stock selection, it is necessary to select stocks in the K-line graph where each of the subsequent peaks and valleys are higher than the previous peaks and valleys (one bottom is higher than the bottom).

The two connected lows with uptrend stocks are connected in turn to arrive at an uptrend line. Usually, the uptrend line plays a supporting role in the stock price. Once the uptrend line is formed, the stock price will run above the trend line for a while. Based on this principle, investors can select stocks above the uptrend line.

In this chapter we have learned a lot of basics of the stock market along with a good indicator of buying a stock. In the next chapter we will dig in deep about this and do many things that can help the stock market to understand you better. Let us dive into it.

# CHAPTER 3

# How to Buy Your First Stock

There are principles for the first stock selection.

Stock investment is a kind of venture investment that combines foresight, profound professional knowledge, wisdom and practical experience. It is especially important to choose stocks that workout well. Investors must analyze carefully and judge independently.

Investors should follow certain principles when selecting stocks.

## 1. Principle of Interests

The principle of interest is the first principle to choose stocks. Investing in stocks is to obtain the long-term return or short-term spread income brought by a stock for its own investment. Investors must proceed from this goal, overcome personal regional concepts or personality preferences, and choose investment varieties. No matter what sector or industry this stock belongs to, any stock that can bring rich returns is the best investment variety.

## 2. Realistic principles

The stock market is unpredictable. The situation of listed companies is changing every year, and the concepts of hot stocks and cold stocks can also be changed due to various situations. Therefore, the choice of stocks mainly depends on the actual performance of the investment varieties. The past history, operating performance and market performance of listed companies can only be used as investment references but not as selection criteria. There is no need for investors to adopt an idea and completely choose their favorite investment varieties in the past.

## 3. The principle of balancing short-term and long-term benefits

Judging from the way of earning income, there are two kinds of investment income in stocks:

The first is mainly the short-term spread income brought to investors from price changes;

The second is the long-term investment income from the development of listed companies and the stock market.

It is possible to miss some varieties with long-term investment value by completely carrying out short-term speculation to seek spread gains. On the contrary, if all investments are made from the perspective of long-term returns, it is possible to miss very favorable investment opportunities in the market. Therefore, when investors select stocks, they should give consideration to both investment methods in order to maximize their investment profits.

## 4. Principle of relative safety

All stocks in the stock market have certain risks, so it is unrealistic to seek absolutely safe stocks. However, investors can still avoid investment varieties with too much risk through careful selection. For the vast majority of small and medium-sized investors if there is absence of accurate information one generally do not participate in the speculation of problem stocks and should choose relatively safe stocks as investment targets to avoid serious problems with listed companies.

For example:

1. Listed companies with serious litigation disputes and company property sealed up by the court.

2. Listed companies with serious losses, debts, insolvency and imminent bankruptcy for several consecutive years.

3. Listed companies that resort to deceit and fabricate false results to obtain listing qualifications, share allotment and additional issuance.

4. Listed companies that fabricate false and annual reports to mislead investors.

5. Listed companies that have committed serious violations and are managed by informed criticism.

6. Special handling companies listed by Securities Regulatory Commission as delisting companies.

The above-mentioned companies are different from listed companies that are generally specially treated (ST). They are not only poor in economic benefits, but also often have serious problems in operation and management. Investing in these stocks may not be effective and can lead to major economic losses.

Investors who participate in the speculation of these stocks are likely to get better returns after these listed companies gain vitality through asset restructuring. However, if these listed companies fail in this attempt, they will eventually be delisted by the Securities Regulatory Commission to stop trading, and the funds invested by investors will also face the danger of losing all their money. Generally speaking, the risks of these stocks are too great, and the majority of small and medium-sized investors should have a clear understanding of this.

## Eight-point Basis for Selecting Shares for the best stock

There are tens of millions of stocks in the market. Even if an investor has abundant funds, it is impossible to buy all the stocks in the market at the same time. How to choose stocks with small risks and large returns for investment is really a difficult task. For small investors with a small amount of capital, it is even more difficult to choose a good investment target among the dazzling large number of stocks. Because of this, there is a analogy that says "stock selection is like a beauty contest". However, stock selection is not without strategy. The following methods are the essence of stock selection.

1. Select shares according to the company's performance

Company performance is the fundamental force of stock price changes. If the company performs well, its stock price will surely keep rising steadily, otherwise it will decline. Therefore, long-term investors should mainly consider the company's performance for stock selection. The most important indicator of a company's performance is earnings per share and its growth rate. According to the current situation of our country's companies, it is generally believed that those with after-tax earnings per share of more than 0.8 dollar and an annual growth rate of more than 25% have long-term investment value.

2. Stock Selection Based on Economic Cycle

The market performance of company stocks in different industries is very different in different stages of the economic cycle. Some companies are extremely sensitive to the impact of changes in the economic cycle. When the economy is prosperous, the company's business develops rapidly and its profits are extremely rich. On the contrary, when the economy is in recession, its performance also drops obviously.

The other kind of companies are not much affected by the economic boom or recession. During the boom, their profits will not increase significantly, and during the recession there will be no obvious decrease or even better. Therefore, during the economic boom, investors had to better choose the former type of stock. When the economy is in recession, it is better to choose the latter type of stock.

### 3. Select shares based on net asset value per share

The net asset value per share is the "gold content" of the stock, which is the intrinsic value of the stock and is the real shareholder's equity in the current assets of the company and exists in the form of real or cash. It is also the internal controlling force of the stock price change. Under normal circumstances, the net asset value per share must be higher than the par value of each stock, but it's usually lower than the market value of the stock because the market value always contains the investors' expectations.

Under a certain market price, the higher the net asset value per share, the more valuable the stock is. Therefore, investors should choose stocks with high net asset value per share to invest. If the market price is lower than the net asset value per share, its investment value is extremely high. Of course, stocks with low net asset value and low market price can also be appropriately selected.

### 4. Select stocks according to the price-earnings ratio of stocks

Price/earnings ratio is a comprehensive index, from which long-term investors can see the current period of stock investment, while short-term investors can observe the level of stock price. Generally speaking, stocks with lower price-earnings ratio should be selected. However, a stock with a long-term low price-earnings ratio may not be worth choosing because it may be an inactive stock that is not favored by most investors, and the market is always determined by popular behavior, so its price may have difficulty rising. There is no absolute standard as to what level the price-earnings ratio is worth choosing. Judging from current economic development and enterprise growth, the price-earnings ratio is not high at about 20.

### 5. Select stocks according to their market performance

The net assets of stocks are the basis of the performance of the stock market, but the two are not completely corresponding, that is, the market price of stocks with high net assets may not have good performance, and the market price of stocks with the same or similar net assets may have great difference. Therefore, for short-term investors, how the market price changes, i.e. its fluctuation range is not large and its rising space is not wide and is also an important basis for stock selection. Generally speaking, short-term operators had better choose those stocks that have a large rise in the short term or a large fluctuation in the market price. These stocks offer greater short-term profit opportunities.

## 6. Select stocks according to personal circumstances

Most investors often have a preference for certain stocks which may be because they are familiar with the company's business of such stocks, or have a more manageable personality of such stocks and are easy to operate, etc. When selecting stocks according to personal circumstances, one should fully consider one's financial, risk, psychological, time, knowledge and other aspects of affordability. For example, some stocks are subject to frequent ups and downs and volatility, so they are not suitable for investors who are not able to afford the above.

## 7. Select stocks according to whether the stock price increase is ahead of schedule or not

Usually the best two or three stocks in the same industry will have a strong trend while other stocks are struggling. The former is called "leading stock" while the latter is called "sympathy stock". Leading stocks are also stocks that have advanced gains and should be chosen by investors.

## How do you find these lead stocks?

A simple method is to measure the relative price intensity of stocks. The so-called "relative price intensity" refers to the ratio of the price increase of a certain stock in a certain period to the price index or the increase of other stocks in the same period. It is generally believed that stocks with relative price intensity above 80 are of great selection value.

### 8. Select stocks according to the four market segments of the bull market.

The trend of the bull market can be generally divided into four segments:

The first segment is a sharp rise in stock prices. The whole market has a huge increase, usually accounting for 50% of the whole bull market. During this period, when most stocks rebound from the excessively depressed level of the short market, almost all stocks will rise. During this period, you can try high-risk stocks. When the short market turns and the threat of corporate bankruptcy decreases, these stocks will return to a more normal level and their growth will have a good performance.

The second segment of the market is also quite favorable, with the share price index rising more than 25% of the overall bull market. In general, growth stocks begin to perform well during this period. Investors generally see the beautiful future of economic development and look for ways to participate in growth. In this investment climate, growth stocks will rise in price faster, and the trend of blue-chip growth stocks at this time is also quite good, which may rise even higher than the stock price index. Therefore, in this period of market, it is best to choose growth stocks of blue chips.

The increase in the third segment is obviously smaller, generally less than 25% of the overall bull market, and only very limited stocks continue to rise. The possible strategies for this market segment are: sell the second-class growth stocks slowly and transfer part of the funds to the blue-chip growth stocks with the ability to maintain the price level in the multi-head market, and purchase those stocks that conform to the trend and can especially benefit from future economic difficulties. In short, preparations must be made for the short market within this period.

The fourth segment of the market is the end of the multi-head market. At this time, all the stocks that should have risen have already risen about the same. Only the high-performance growth stocks and a few stocks that can profit from the economic difficulties can continue to rise. Therefore, the stock selection for this period of market is the most difficult and usually it is time to prepare to withdraw from the market. However, it is difficult to determine when the short market will come. Therefore, it is not wise to liquidate all the short markets at this time. The best safeguard is to maintain some outstanding growth stocks instead of taking short positions.

## Competitive Advantage Shares

Modern society is a competitive society. In the market economy, listed companies also need to survive and develop in the market competition. Some of these companies with their large scale, strong strength and excellent competitive ability, have formed their superior positions in the market by means of buying mergers and other means.

The competitiveness of listed companies is closely related to their business operations. The competitiveness of listed companies is often manifested by their advantages in scale, good product quality, high operating efficiency, innovative technology, familiarity with market conditions, attention to product demand dynamics, good marketing skills, etc. Investors who invest in companies with competitive advantages wlll naturally have good returns.

Because only a long-term and sustained competitive advantage can create a good long-term development prospect for the company, and also can make an excellent company with evergreen foundation.

The competitive position of listed companies in the same trade is strong or weak, and the evaluation criteria are as follows.

1. Examining the annual sales volume or annual income of listed companies is an important criterion to measure a company's relative competitive position in the same industry. It is better reflected by the proportion of company sales volume in the total industry sales volume.

In the fierce competition in the same industry, the company that accounts for a large proportion of the total sales must be a company with strong competitiveness. The company's profit mainly comes from sales revenue. The larger the revenue, the more the profit. Therefore, investors should first choose the leading listed companies in the industry.

2. Examine the growth of sales or income

The ideal investment target for investors is not limited to famous listed companies, but also goes to those listed companies with considerable scale and rapid growth in sales because rapid expansion is more important than large scale. High growth in sales often leads to high growth in profits, thus increasing the company's stock price and dividends and achieving the expected benefits of investors in stock investment.

3. Examine the stability of sales

Under normal circumstances, stable sales revenue is accompanied by relatively stable profits. If the sales revenue varies from time to time and changes too much, it will not only bring great disadvantages to the operation and management of listed companies. But there is a chance that it will increase the uncertainty of dividends and bonuses paid to shareholders. Therefore, investors should pay full attention to the growth stability of the company in their choices.

Hope this chapter helped you in choosing the best stock according to your interest. In the next chapter we will discuss some strategies that can be used to advance your level in trading and investing.

# CHAPTER 4

# BASIC STRATEGIES IN THE STOCK MARKET

Just as the stock market is a noisy and restless sea, the operation of an enterprise is not calm. To understand whether a stock and company is doing well or not you need to carefully follow what is happening around. This list will help you create a clear-cut strategy about a share. Follow further to know more about these. A listed company always grows with various sudden and influential events. Major events commonly seen in enterprises include the following.

## 1. The company entered into a major contract

The contract may have a significant impact on one or more of the company's assets, liabilities, rights and interests and operating results. In the contract, the most common is the sales contract about products or services. In the production and operation of an enterprise, the most important thing is to ensure that the products or services it produces are marketable.

If there is no market for its products or services, the most advanced technological equipment and scientific production organizations will be wasted.

The conclusion of the sales contract will ensure the sale of products or services for a period of time in the future and can ensure the acquisition of operating income, enable the production and sales of enterprises to continue, and thus ensure the survival and development of enterprises.

For example, some listed companies often disclose that the company's sales contract has been booked for the next two years, which strongly indicates that the products provided by the company are in a state of short supply, and investors have reason to believe that the survival of the company will not have problems in the next two years.

## 2. Shareholders' General Meeting and Resolutions

According to regulations, the shareholders' meeting must be held at least once a year. At the shareholders' meeting, members of the board of directors and the board of supervisors are usually re-elected. The changes of these senior management personnel will definitely affect the company's management style and level. The relevant resolutions of the shareholders' meeting, such as authorization to the board of directors, changes to investment projects, plans for increasing capital and shares and profit distribution, will also affect the vital interests of the company's investors.

3. Major changes in the company's operating policies or operating projects

There is no doubt that major changes in the company's operating policies, operating methods and operating items will affect the company's future operating results, and even affect the company's survival and development.

4. The company has made major investments or purchased long-term assets with a large amount of money.

Major investment behavior of the company, or the purchase of long-term assets with large amount, will affect the change of shareholders' rights and interests. If the investment fails, the net assets of the company will be reduced and the net assets per share will be reduced. In the past few years, some listed companies have not performed well and out of this a considerable part of which is caused by unreasonable or blind investment.

5. The company incurred significant debts

Generally speaking, enterprises need to borrow money frequently in their operations to ensure the turnover of funds. Although some companies never borrow money, it is an important skill for enterprises to use borrowing flexibly to speed up the turnover of funds. However, if the company has too much debt and its asset-liability ratio remain high, approaching or even reaching 100%, the company will face the danger of bankruptcy. Therefore, investors must pay close attention to the major debts incurred by the company.

### 6. The company suffered heavy losses in assets.

In the operation of an enterprise, there are two types of events that easily lead to the loss of the company's assets, one is natural disasters, the other is man-made. Natural disasters are some irresistible natural forces, such as floods, earthquakes, etc. Man-made disasters are mainly investment mistakes, man-made operational mistakes in production, etc.

When the company's assets suffer losses, first, it is necessary to study how much weight the lost assets have compared with the company's net assets and how much influence they have on the net assets per share. The second is its impact on the future management of the enterprise, whether it will affect the production, and how long the enterprise can resume production, so as to make a reasonable forecast of the operating benefits in the future years.

### 7. Default of the Company's Failure to Pay Major Debt Due

When the debt is due, the company's failure to pay major debt indicates that the company's capital turnover is difficult and may affect the operation of the enterprise. For example, a department store borrowed a large amount of money by using its business premises as collateral, but due to its failure to fulfill its debts when due, financial institutions filed a lawsuit with the court, demanding that the premises of the department store be auctioned. The department store was unable to continue its business due to the loss of its business premises and eventually went bankrupt.

8. The newly promulgated laws, regulations, policies and rules may have a significant impact on the company's operation.

The company's operation will be affected not only by its operation level and environment, but also by relevant laws and regulations. For example, in order to protect the environment, the state stipulates that some low-grade and small-scale paper mills must stop production or add sewage treatment devices within a specified period of time, which is bound to increase the production cost of paper mills or directly affect the survival of paper mills.

If the state grants "national treatment" to foreign-invested enterprises, at the same time, all enterprises will be treated equally in terms of income tax, and no enterprise shall be special. Then, at present, the preferential income tax rate of 15% enjoyed by some listed companies will be canceled, and the net profit will be reduced under the same total profit.

9. Shareholders who hold more than 5% of the company's ordinary shares issued outside the company, and the increase or decrease of the shares held by them reach more than 2% of the total amount of the shares issued outside the company.

According to the regulations of Securities Regulatory Commission, when the increase or decrease of the ordinary shares held more than 5% of the shares issued outside the company reach more than 2% of the total amount of the shares issued outside the company, it means that the major shareholders of the company increase or decrease the company's shares. If the shareholding is increased, there may be an acquisition event, while the reduction of the company's shares may change the structure of major shareholders, thus affecting the composition of the board of directors.

10. Major changes have taken place in the company's production and operation environment.

Major changes in the company's operating environment will have an impact on the company's operations. Another example is that if the company moves to the development zone or registers in the development zone, it will enable the company to enjoy preferential income tax, thus affecting the retention of the company's after-tax profits. For example, the improvement of communication and transportation conditions in the company's locality can speed up the communication of business information and shorten the transportation time of raw materials and products, thus helping the company to improve its business level.

## 11. The chairman of the board of directors, more than 30% of the directors have changed or the general manager has changed.

When the chairman of the board of directors or more than 30% of the directors change or the general manager changes, it means that the company's senior management and decision-making level have changed, and the company's operating policies and so on may be affected and changed.

## 12. Changes to the Articles of Association, Registered Capital and Registered Address of the Company

Changes in the company's articles of association, registered capital and address indicate changes in the company's operating strength, mode of operation or operating environment.

## 13. Major litigation events involving the company

Major lawsuits involving the company may affect the company's survival and development. If a listed company has two loan guarantees that have entered the litigation stage before listing, but the listed company believes that it is reasonable that it should not be the defendant and fails to notify the shareholders. As a result, after losing the lawsuit, the listed company was found to be jointly and severally liable for the loan. Because the guaranteed person could not fulfill the repayment obligation, the listed company would be responsible for paying the principal and interest of the loan of nearly 40 million dollars on behalf of the guaranteed person, thus causing major losses to the shareholders of the listed company.

### 14. The company has entered a state of liquidation and bankruptcy.

The liquidation and bankruptcy of the company indicate that the company's operation has come to an end. This is definitely something investors should pay attention to.

### 15. The issuance of bonds or shares by a company

The company has issued bonds or shares to the outside world. While raising funds and enhancing the company's operating strength, it also changes the company's asset-liability structure and equity structure, thus affecting the company's operation.

16. The mortgage, sale or retirement of the company's main operating assets exceed 30% of the total assets

The mortgage, sale or scrapping of the company's operating assets will affect the normal operation of the company's production and operation.

## 17. Merger or division of the company

The merger of the company with other companies or the division of the company itself will affect the division of the company's property and the way of operation, thus affecting the company's survival and further development.

These major events will have a profound impact on the company's operation and management, thus changing the operating performance of listed companies. The stock market is a market where speculation is prevalent. Every major event in a listed company will become the subject of stock speculation and the trigger for a change in stock price. Depending on the type of "event" or "news," the price may rise or fall.

It can be said that the major events of listed companies definitely breed "dark horses".

In this chapter we have learned a lot about strategies and points to see when trying to invest in stock markets. Next two chapters will help us to understand the process of analysis in stock markets. Let us dive into it.

# CHAPTER 5

# Analyzing Stock Markets

Looking at the market from the distance mainly refers to analyzing the trend of the market from the fundamentals of stock investment, including major macroeconomic emergencies and industry situations, etc. These fundamentals are closely related to the rise and fall of stock prices and will be introduced separately in this chapter.

## Overview of Fundamental Analysis Methods

Fundamental analysis, also known as basic analysis and is based on the intrinsic value of securities and focuses on the analysis of various factors that affect the price and trend of securities. This in detail determine what kind of securities to invest in and when to buy them. The main contents of fundamental analysis are shown in this chapter.

The premise of the basic analysis is that the price of

securities is determined by its intrinsic value, and the price changes frequently under the influence of many factors such as politics, economy, psychology, etc. It is difficult to be completely consistent with the value, but it always fluctuates around the value. Rational investors should make investment decisions according to the relationship between securities price and value.

The basic analysis of the stock market mainly focuses on the research and analysis of the company from the fundamental factors of the stock, such as macro-economy, industry background, enterprise management ability, financial situation, etc. We should try to find out the "intrinsic value" of the stock from the perspective of the company, thus comparing with the stock market value, and selecting the stock with the most investment value.

The relationship between value investment and fundamental analysis is so harmonious that it can be said that there is no value investment without fundamental analysis. It is the most basic cornerstone of value investment, or the vast majority of work of value investment is to do fundamental analysis.

### Analysis 1: Using Macroeconomic Information

Major changes in the economic situation will have a direct impact on the stock market, and the stock market's response will be more obvious. For example, in different economic stages, the state will promulgate different relevant tax policies, industrial policies and monetary policies.

## Impact of GDP on Stock Market

GDP (Gross Domestic Product) refers to the market value of all final products (goods and services) produced by economic society (I.e. a country or region) using production factors within a certain period of time, that is, GDP. It is a measure of the total amount of final products produced by all resident units in a country's (region's) economy during the accounting period, and is often regarded as an important indicator showing a country's (region's) economic situation.

The decline or growth of GDP can be reflected in the rise and fall of the market index, thus affecting the trend of all individual stocks. The sharp growth of GDP reflects the vigorous economic development of the region.

The relationship between GDP and stock price is as follows:

During the period of economic prosperity enterprises run well and make more profits and stock price rises. When the economy is in recession, corporate profits decline and stock prices weaken. That is, when GDP or the added value of related industries is on the rise, it is a good time to choose stocks.

Step 1 is the GDP comparison data from the first

quarter of 2013 to the second quarter of 2014.

Step 2, as described is the chart of Google Composite Index K from the first quarter of 2013 to the second quarter of 2014.

Step 3 As shown is, due to the overall decline in the market, many individual stocks also showed a trend of overall decline during the first quarter of 2014.

### Impact of Inflation on Stock Market

Inflation Risk is also called "purchasing power risk" and refers to the possibility that the bank's cost increases or its actual income decreases due to inflation factors. When inflation occurs, the nominal income of the joint-stock company will increase due to the increase in the price of the company's products.

Especially when the increase in the price of the company's products is larger than the increase in production costs, the company's net profit will increase. At this time, the dividend will increase, and the stock price will also increase. Common shareholders will receive higher income, which can partially mitigate the losses caused by inflation. However, it should be pointed out that the impact of inflation risk on different stocks is different.

For example, from the mid-1970s to the 1980s, U.S. companies managed to increase their earnings per share to a level roughly equivalent to the inflation rate (about 10%). However, in order to protect shareholder value, these enterprises must actually increase their profit growth rate to about 20%. This gap was one of the main reasons for the weak stock market returns in those years.

## Effect of Interest Rate on Stock Market

Interest Rates, also known as interest rates, are indicators to measure the level of interest and the ratio of the amount of interest to the principal in a certain period of time. The calculation formula is: interest rate = interest/principal.

Interest rate is an important economic indicator that affects the market. In times of economic depression, lowering interest rate can stimulate economic development, while in times of inflation, rising interest rate can inhibit vicious economic development. Usually, the rise and fall of interest rate is inversely proportional to the change of stock price.

It should be noted that the interest rate is not absolutely inversely proportional to the change of stock price. In some special circumstances, when the market is soaring, the adjustment of interest rate has little effect on the control of stock price. Similarly, when the market plummets, even if there is an adjustment policy of interest rate reduction, it may make the stock price recover weakly.

## Impact of Economic Cycle on Stock Market

Business cycle is also called business cycle, business cycle and prosperity cycle. It refers to a phenomenon that economic expansion and economic contraction alternate and alternate periodically in economic operation. It is the fluctuation of gross national output, gross income and gross employment.

The economic cycle can be divided into four stages: prosperity, recession, depression and recovery. For different types of industries, their degree of influence by the economic cycle is also different.

[Experts Remind]

In modern macroeconomics, the economic cycle occurs when real GDP rises (expands) or falls (shrinks or declines) and is relative to potential GDP. Every economic cycle can be divided into two stages: rising and falling. The rising phase is also called prosperity, and the highest point is called peak. An economy that goes from peak to peak, or from valley to valley, is a complete economic cycle.

## Influence of Deposit Reserve Ratio on Stock Market

Deposit reserve, also known as statutory deposit reserve or deposit reserve, refers to the deposits in the central bank prepared by financial institutions to ensure the withdrawal of deposits by customers and the needs of capital settlement. The ratio of the deposit reserve required by the central bank to its total deposit is the deposit-reserve ratio, which is often used by the central bank to regulate the macroeconomic operation.

The deposit reserve ratio will affect the interest rate, and the interest rate will affect the price of securities. Generally speaking, as the deposit reserve ratio rises, interest rates will be under pressure to rise which is a sign of tightening monetary policy. The deposit reserve ratio is aimed at banks and other financial institutions and has an indirect impact on end customers. Interest rates are aimed at end customers, such as the interest on your deposits, and the impact is direct.

The adjustment of the statutory reserve ratio has a greater impact on the economy and is prone to adverse consequences. Therefore, western countries have gradually weakened its role and set a very low or even zero statutory reserve ratio. However, central bank frequently uses this monetary policy tool, with 10 times in 2007 and 9 times in 2008.

## Effect of Exchange Rate on Stock Market

Exchange rate is also called "foreign exchange market or exchange rate", which refers to the ratio of one country's currency to another country's currency, and is the price of another currency expressed in one currency. Due to the different names and currencies of different countries in the world, one country's currency has to set a rate of exchange that is the exchange rate, against the currencies of other countries.

Exchange rate is an important adjustment lever in international trade. Because the cost of goods produced by a country is calculated in its own currency, the cost of goods must be related to the exchange rate to compete in the international market. The exchange rate also directly affects the cost and price of the commodity in the international market and directly affects the international competitiveness of the commodity.

Under normal circumstances, the rise and fall of the stock market is a manifestation of the relationship between supply and demand, and there are many factors that affect the relationship between supply and demand. On the exchange rate issue alone, generally speaking, an increase in a country's exchange rate for foreign currencies will lead to more foreign currencies being exchanged for local currencies and promote the demand for local currencies.

Monetary policy is one of the basic means for the government to control macro-economy. Since the balance between the total social supply and demand and the balance between the total money supply and the total money demand complement each other, the focus of macroeconomic regulation must be based on the money supply. Monetary policy focuses on the adjustment and control of money supply, thus achieving macroeconomic goals such as stabilizing money, increasing employment, balancing international payments, and developing the economy.

For an open market, the exchange of foreign currency for local currency will likely enter the stock market, thus increasing the source of capital for the stock market and prompting the stock to appreciate. On the other hand, when there is no central bank to raise foreign currency, a large loss of local currency will lead to the flow of stock market funds to foreign exchange markets, causing the stock market to fall; or vice versa.

## Impact of Price Changes on Stock Market

Generally speaking, the price is actually the production price, and the production price is the price composed of the average production cost of the department and the average profit of the society, and the production price is the transformation form of the value. Price changes have an important impact on the stock market.

## Influence of Political Factors on Stock Market

Politics and economy are closely linked. If international political activities with greater influence occur, they will usually have greater influence on the international economic situation, thus causing stock prices to fluctuate. From the domestic point of view, if the state adjusts and changes its political policies, or if economic policies with wide influence and relevant laws and regulations are promulgated, the stock price will also be obviously affected.

The occurrence of major international political events will directly lead to obvious fluctuations in stock prices. Investors can judge the stock price trends of relevant companies according to different political situations, thus adopting corresponding investment strategies.

## Influence of Natural Factors on Stock Market

The impact of natural disasters on stock prices results from the damage of disasters to physical assets. When disasters occur, production is affected and stock prices fall. On the other hand, post-disaster reconstruction stimulates the expansion of production and the stock prices of related industries will rise to a certain extent.

For example, from 2002 to 2003, although the direct losses caused by stocks were not large, they seriously affected people's normal production and life, and some industries suffered serious losses. The state has made a major strategic decision to "not relax in the prevention and treatment of with one hand and not waver in the economic construction center with the other". It has increased its support for agriculture and rural economy, small and medium-sized enterprises, service industries and other industries that have been greatly affected by this. Under the effective macro-policy control, the negative impact of this on the stock market has been effectively controlled. After the growth rate temporarily dropped to 6.7% in the second quarter of 2003, it quickly recovered to 9.1% in the third quarter.

## Analysis 2: Using Industry Information

Although macro-economic factors have great influence on the stock market, under the same economic situation, the analysis of the industry situation is also very important to see the market.

### Classification of Industries

Changes in the industry's position in the national economy, the industry's development prospects and potential, the impact of emerging industries, as well as the position of listed companies in the industry, operating results, operating conditions, changes in capital mix and changes in leadership personnel will all affect the prices of relevant stocks.

The subject of our research is the factors that affect the stock because the stock is the financing platform of the industry. It can make the industry have greater development and therefore, different industries have different impacts on the stock.

In the stock market, the industries are classified as

- agriculture, forestry, animal husbandry and fishery,
- mining; manufacturing; production and supply of electricity, gas and water;

- construction; transportation, warehousing and postal services;
- information transmission, computer services and software industry;
- wholesale and retail trade; accommodation and catering;
- Finance; real estate; leasing and business services;
- scientific research, technical services and geological exploration;
- water conservancy, environment and public facilities management industry; i) resident services and other services;
- education; health, social security and social welfare; culture, sports and entertainment;
- public administration and social organizations.

## Nature of Industry

The nature of the industry is to divide most of the industries in the society theoretically, and to divide the categories of different industries, such as manufacturing industry, service industry, agriculture, etc., and according to the businesses engaged in in the industry and the degree of contribution to the society.

## Life Cycle of Industry

The curve shape of the Industry life cycle and the curve shape of the product life cycle are approximately the same, both of which are S-shaped and all pass through four stages: that is the introduction stage, the growth stage, the maturity stage and the decline stage (or the metamorphosis stage).

There is no obvious boundary in each stage of the industry's life cycle. Only by judging the arrival of a new stage of the industry sensitively and making corresponding strategic preparations in advance can we be in an advantageous position in the competition.

There are significant differences in enterprise behaviors in different industry life cycles, such as enterprise strategy, enterprise capability, organizational structure, investment and risk, enterprise reorganization and merger, competitive behavior, etc. It can be seen that different strategies should be formulated to invest in different stages of enterprise stocks.

At the same time in different life cycle stages of the industry, its stock prices usually also show the same characteristics. so according to the above analysis of the life cycle of enterprises in a certain industry, investors can analyze the rise and fall of the stock and its future value, and then invest more accurately.

## Methods of Industry Analysis

When making fundamental analysis, investors should first consider the large economic environment, then examine the current situation of the industry, and finally the company. Industry is a bridge between macro-economy and economy. When stocks are traded, we can infer one thing or two from the status of the industry, such as industrial revitalization planning or the establishment of an inflection point in the industry. Major policies or obvious recovery in the industry will lead to the activation of the sector, thus helping investors to grasp the hot sectors.

In general, investors can obtain all kinds of industry information from the network and life.

1. Network: Large financial websites that regularly provide up-to-date information and industry research and analysis reports.

2. Life: In daily life, investors also need to pay more attention to the industries around them. For example, you can pay attention to agriculture when you buy vegetables, retail when you shop in supermarkets, finance when you deposit or withdraw money from banks, and real estate when you see the construction of surrounding buildings. Investors can also pay attention to the industry in which they work, know the industry data regularly published by some large websites, and judge the development of the industry. These experiences need to accumulate over time.

Market analysis of the industry involves the company's core competitiveness, which is also the company's "safety barrier". Some companies master core technologies and some companies are monopolies, which will continuously generate huge profits and will not be duplicated and lead to overcapacity. However, this does not mean that such companies are definitely worth investing in, and depends on the price of the company.

## Analysis of the Company's Management Ability

For a specific individual stock, the main factors that affect its price level lie in the internal quality of the enterprise itself including a series of factors such as financial situation, operating conditions, management level, technical ability, market size, industry characteristics, development potential, etc. Enterprises are the main body of the market economy.

Understanding enterprises and doing a good job in enterprises are the issues that investors, lenders, managers and management departments are most concerned about.

The following is an introduction to the operation method of analyzing the management ability of listed companies.

Among the microeconomic factors that affect stock price fluctuations, listed companies are the main factors that determine their own stock prices.

1. Company performance.

The company's performance is mainly reflected in various financial indicators of the company. The main factors affecting the company's performance include the company's net assets, profit level, dividend pay-out, share splitting and expansion, capital increase and reduction, and turnover. Generally speaking, the profitability of the company, the profitability of the company and the profit situation of the company are the fundamental factors that determine the stock price of the company.

2. The growth of the company.

The company's growth is also the company's ability to expand its operations. Analysis of the company's growth is a judgment of the company's development prospects and focuses not on short-term stock price fluctuations, but on the long-term benefits of investment in the company's stock.

3. Asset reorganization and acquisition.

This is a major organizational change made by listed companies to realize scale benefits or turn losses into profits through merger and reorganization. Many large and medium-sized state-owned listed companies with losses or small profits in our country have realized the adjustment and transformation of industrial structure through asset restructuring. At present, the modes of asset restructuring mainly include asset replacement, high-quality asset injection and non-performing asset stripping. The acquisition of listed companies is the most dynamic phenomenon in the stock market, and the acquisition of listed companies is often accompanied by a sharp rise in stock prices.

Here we have discussed a lot about analyzing in this chapter. In the next chapter we will further enhance our skills and improve them. Let us learn about them in detail in the next chapters. Go move!

# CHAPTER 6

# Advanced Analysis to Pick Right Stocks

## Technical Analysis

The price of the securities market is complex, and investors have a set of methods to develop or choose investment strategies in the market. Technical analysis is the most important technique to understand how a stock is performing. Technical analysis can also be used to predict the future or expectations of a stock. We will look about all of them in detail in the coming sections. Let us dive into it.

### Framework Technical Analysis Methods

The technical analysis is referred to as the market behavior as the research object to determine the market trends and follow the trend of the periodic changes in the sum of the stock and all financial derivative transaction decisions. Technical analysis makes us understand that the market behavior is in digestion. The maintenance of the stock analysis investment is mainly three, that is, basic analysis, technical analysis, evolution analysis.

Among them, the basic analysis is mainly used in the selection of the investment analysis and the cost of the analysis of the effective and effectiveness of the investment analysis, as an important means of improving the effectiveness and reliability of the investment analysis. Everyone's focus on the future, worried, fear, etc., is concentrated in the stock price and trading volume.

### Analysis 1:

Use K-wire technology to analyze K-line said that originated in the 18th century Japanese Mekhi, when the meter of Japan's merchandise to indicate the change of price of the price, after the referred to the securities market, as a theory of stock technical analysis. We will discuss about in detail in this section.

Base of the basic morphology K-line diagram shows the technical analysis of the price change in the unit time period and is used to sell the various stocks daily, weekly, monthly discount price, closing price, highest price, minimum price and other sharp changes. The graphics is shown in the pattern of the drawing, and the addition of these candles have a black and white, which also known as the binasalstyle chart.

First, the first day or a period of time is found to be a larger and lowest price, and then find the day and a period of time and the market, and the two orders of the next day and the re-market, and then the two orders of the line and the price of the re-shaped, and the two-dimensional rectangle is connected to a narrow long-sided cylinder.

K-analysis can be easily analyzed using single meaning structure that is available for analysis. It can be used to understand previous days fluctuations and stock price changes. By using this data one can easily understand the wave that stock market is dealing with at that particular time. Apart from this k-line is used for technical analysis of intra-day trading and options trading.

It should be noted that the stock price may vary in different price points. We will look at different parameters that will help the stock price to deviate and absorb. Similarly, we will try to clone the k-line and understand its basic advantages. There is also a high chance of one making low opting points based on k-line description. It is however very well understood that k-line is one of the important technical analysis tools that is available and if used well can help investors achieve their financial independence that they dream of.

- Master the line of K

Some typical K-line or K-line combination will continue to repeat. if investors have grasped these laws it will increase investment grangers. Here is some common K-line combination.

- Wear junction:

This is the combination of two knag lines (kin) lines and understands bounds of the K-line. It is called the image of the shock amplification and can be accepted as the change of the transitional deviation.

- Shortage:

Appearance of the line and other casual lines can be fallen into this category. The combination of the two k-line combination of the K-line is destined and fell to encounter tenacious resistance and can attain long-term reacting strength.

- Cover:

This is the largest number of stocks, and the more sharply the larger the value of the transformation of the shaft, the more sharply the largest. The larger the price of the transformation of the sharp line must be a round of the decline in the next day, the number of the majority of the sun can be used to carry out the next day of the open line

- Cross:

This is the combination of two Kang Long and the presence of the situation of the two-line using different methodologies. The display of the original movement trend and can be decided that the market is brewing.

## Points for Attention in K-line Analysis

K-line chart is one of the charts that can best show the market behavior. However, some common K-line combinations do not have strict scientific logic. Therefore, attention should be paid to the problems shown when applying K-line.

In order to have a deeper understanding of K-line combination forms, the internal and external principles of each combination form should be understood. Because it is not a perfect technology, this is the same as other technical analysis methods. K-line analysis is established by human subjective impression and is one of the analysis methods based on the expression of historical morphological combination. By using this analysis one can easily make things better and choose good stocks that will give a good return of investment. It is recommended to follow a lot of newsletter articles so that the trader will have a sufficient knowledge on what is going on around the stock prices.

## Analysis 2: Analysis by Trend Line Technology

Trend line is a method of trend analysis. Trend line analysis method is simple and easy to use, and has good effect in judging stock price trend. Using trend line can simply and clearly grasp the trend of stock price, so as to make the best use of the situation and follow the trend.

### Trend Line

The most important investment principle of actual investors is to follow the trend of the stock price running along the direction of minimum resistance, and to achieve "harmony between heaven and man" with the trend of stock price fluctuation.

The concept of trend mainly refers to the direction of stock price movement. It is the embodiment of the orderly characteristics of stock price fluctuation and the main performance of the biased characteristics in the random fluctuation of stock price. Trends can be divided into long-term trends, medium-term trends and short-term trends according to the length of time. A long-term trend generally consists of several medium-term trends, while a medium-term trend consists of several short-term trends.

The so-called "one ruler goes all over the world" actually refers to the application of trend lines. Investors should always remember that the trend is your friend, always follow the trend and do not act against it. Learning to use trend lines to determine the direction of trends is one of the essential basic skills for investors.

In a price movement, if the peaks and troughs it contains are correspondingly higher than the previous peaks and troughs, then it is called an upward trend. On the contrary, if the wave crest and wave trough it contains are lower than the previous wave crest and wave trough, then it is called downward trend. If the later peaks and troughs are basically the same as the previous peaks and troughs, then it is called oscillation trend, or horizontal trend, or no trend.

## Pipeline Line

Pipeline line is also called channel line or track-line, which is a method to further describe the trend and judge the entry and exit points based on trend line. Pipeline line can also be divided into ascending channel and descending channel. Pipeline line is actually the parallel line of ascending and descending trend line.

Since the pipeline line is composed of upper and lower two lines, it is more specific than a single trend line at the buying and selling point, and the judgment principle of all trend lines is also applicable to the pipeline line. In addition, the advantages of the pipeline line are clear buying and selling points which have fewer transactions and high success rate.

## Support Line and Pressure Line

Support pressure line is a commonly used reference index in stock technical analysis. When the price breaks through the support pressure line, the market may reverse. The support line and the pressure line can be transformed into each other. After breaking through the pressure line, the pressure line is transformed into the support line. Similarly, after breaking through the support line, the support line will be transformed into a pressure line, which conforms to the principle that everything must be reversed.

When the stock price falls near a certain price, the stock price stops falling and may even recover. The price that prevents the stock price from falling further or temporarily prevents the stock price from falling further is the position of the support line. When the stock price rises near a certain price, the stock price will stop rising or even fall back. The price that prevents or temporarily prevents the stock price from continuing to rise is the position of the pressure line.

The function of the support line and the pressure line is to prevent or temporarily prevent the stock price from continuing to move in one direction. At the same time, the support line and the pressure line have the possibility of completely preventing the stock price from changing in the original direction. The role of support and pressure is not the same, they can transform each other. Of course, the premise is to be broken through by effective and strong price changes.

## Inverted Form

The graph of reversal pattern indicates that the original trend of stock price will be reversed, that is, the original trend direction of stock price will be changed. For example, the original upward trend will become a downward trend, or the original downward trend will become an upward trend. The typical figures of reversed shape include double top shape, head shoulder shape, straight line shape and V shape, etc. The following mainly introduces several common reversal patterns.

### 1. v-shaped and inverted v-shaped

Both V-shaped and inverted V-shaped reversal patterns are common in actual combat and are extremely strong. They often occur when the market fluctuates violently. There is only one low point or high point in the bottom or top region of the price where the original running trend is changed, and the stock price shows drastic changes in the opposite direction. V-shaped reversal refers to the stock price falling all the way first, then climbing all the way up, with the bottom at the sharp end, which is like the English letter V on the graph. The inverted V refers to the stock price rising all the way first, then falling all the way, with its head pointed.

V-shape and inverted V-shape have no definite buying and selling point. The best buying point for V-shape is at the initial stage when the low volume cannot fall down and pick up, or when the volume is high and the sun is turning. The inverted V-shaped selling point is the initial stage when the high-level volume rises but does not fall back, or when the high-level volume is large and the negative trend turns.

## 2. Arc top and arc bottom

Circular arc top and circular arc bottom are two common reversal patterns. Investors and market analysts all attach great importance to their research and judgment. In the head-shoulder reversal pattern, the stock price fluctuates greatly, reflecting the fierce struggle between the multi-player and the short-player. After breaking through the neck-line, the shape was established. However, the shape of the circular arc top and the circular arc bottom is a gradual process. Both sides of the market are close to each other, winning alternately so that the stock price will maintain a long period of consolidation before an upward or downward reversal will finally occur.

### (1) Circular Arc Top:

The circular arc top refers to the dome trend of the stock price or stock index. When the stock price reaches the high point, the rise slows down and then gradually declines. It is a peak figure, which indicates that the future market is about to fall. The completion of the whole form takes a long time and often appears in combination with other forms.

After the market rises in the wave band with the buyer's strength slightly stronger than the seller's strength in the initial stage, the buying power weakens while the seller's strength and quantity continuously strengthen. In the medium term, the strength of both sides is balanced, and the volatility of the stock price is very small at this time. In the later period, the strength of the seller exceeds that of the buyer, and the stock price falls back. When it breaks through the neck-line downward, it will drop rapidly.

(2) Circular arc bottom:

Circular arc bottom refers to an arc-shaped upside-down form at the bottom, also known as bowl shape, with stock prices mostly in low-level areas. The similarity with the underlying market is that trading is light and takes several months or even longer, which reflects the typical characteristics of weak market and the extreme lack of investor confidence in the technical trend during the market decline.

The energy in this space and time is basically released. However, due to the strong lethality of the early decline, it is difficult for buyers to pool their buying energy in a short period of time and cannot quickly get out of the bottom to rise. Only by staying at the bottom for a long time to rest all the while exchanging time for space and slowly recovering this can be changed. Normally The price is stuck in a stalemate and the amplitude is very small, thus forming a circular arc bottom.

### 3. Double top and double bottom

There are two special reversal patterns in the K-line combination, namely double top (M-head or double head) and double bottom (W-bottom or double bottom). They appear more frequently in stock market and have great influence. Among them, M-head indicates that there is a possibility of a peak in the future market, which is a signal that the stock price is about to fall. On the other hand, the bottom of W is just the opposite, which indicates that the stock price is about to rise.

No matter M head or W bottom, the breakthrough of neck-line is the effective symbol. Bears see the city is full of tops, but they all have m heads. Any rebound is a good opportunity to ship. However, market is bottomed out everywhere. What do you think is the bottom of W? Any pullback is the time to buy. It is very important to correctly identify the double top and double bottom shapes. This will help stock markets work better.

### Persistent Form

Persistent pattern refers to temporary recuperation during the operation of unilateral trend (falling or rising). The stock price has returned to its original trend after staged recuperation.

Persistent forms are mainly divided into the following 6 types: triangular form, rectangular form, flag form, wedge form, head and shoulder bottom form, irregular form, etc. No matter what type of sustained form it is, as long as its characteristics, volume-price relationship, price measurement space, etc. are understood, it can be properly operated, and the author will not elaborate one by one.

Sustained form is the surest way to generate trading opportunities in operation because sustained form itself embodies the essence of homeopathic operation. At the same time, through its own risk control function, investors can easily control trading risks within a limited range. At the same time, investors can also generate reasonable minimum target prediction through relay form. If assisted by technical means such as moving average and trend line, the trading success rate can reach a high position.

## Analysis 3: Analysis by Index Technology

In order to better predict the future trend of stock prices and the right time to buy and sell stocks, many methods have been produced through people's continuous research on the trend of stock prices. At present, most investors use technical analysis and basic analysis to predict the trend of the stock market. The following describes commonly used technical analysis indicators.

## Average

Averages are all called moving averages (MA). It is a technical analysis method based on Dow Jones's "average cost concept" and using the principle of "moving average" in statistics to connect the average value of stock prices over a period of time into a curve to show the historical fluctuation of stock prices and further reflect the future development trend of stock price indexes.

Average Difference Index (DMA) is a trend index and also a trend analysis index. DMA is a technical analysis index to analyze the price trend according to the difference between fast- and slow-moving average lines. Average difference index mainly judges the current buying and selling energy and the future price trend by calculating the difference between two moving average lines with different reference periods.

The principle of moving average difference index is that when the solid line crosses the dotted line upward it is regarded as the buying point, and when the solid line crosses the dotted line downward, it is the selling point. According to this rule, investors can get that when the solid line crosses the dotted line from the high level twice, the stock price may fall deeper.

When the solid line crosses the dotted line from the low position twice, the stock price may rise by a large margin.

The average difference index is calculated by DMA☐ = short-term average-long-term average, AMA☐ = short-term average. For example, the DMA index taking the 5th and 10th as reference periods is calculated as follows: DMA (5) = 5 -10 day average, AMA(10)=5 day average. 7.5.2 KDJ index.

Random Index (KDJ) was first created by George Lane. It reflects the strength of the price trend through the volatility of the highest, lowest and closing prices on the same day or in recent days.

KDJ index has 3 curves, namely K-line, D line and J line. Among them, the values of k, d and j range from 0 to 100. When the values of k, d and j are below line 20, they are oversold areas, which are regarded as buying signals. When the values of k, d, and j are above line 80, they are overbought areas, which are regarded as selling signals. When the values of k, d, and j are hovering between lines 20-80, investors should wait and see.

The random index KDJ is calculated with the highest price, lowest price and closing price as the basic data. The K value, D value and J value obtained from a point on the coordinate of the index respectively, and countless such points are connected to form a complete KDJ index that can reflect the price fluctuation trend.

The calculation formula and theory of random index are based on the previously generated immature random value RSV. RSV for n days = (Ct-Ln) ÷ ÷ ÷ (Hn-LN) × 100, where CT in the formula refers to the closing price of the day, HN and LN refer to the highest and lowest prices in the latest n days, including the day.

After exponential smoothing of RSV value, k value can be obtained: k value today = 2/3 × k value yesterday+1/3 RSV value today, where 1/3 in the formula is a smoothing factor and can be selected artificially. Perform exponential smoothing on the k value to obtain the d value.

### BOLL indicator

BOLL was created by John-Bollingcr. It uses statistical principles to find the standard deviation of stock price and its confidence interval, thus determining the fluctuation range and future trend of stock price.

### BOLL

The Bollinger Bands index shows the safe high and low prices of stock prices by using wave bands. Therefore, it is called Bollinger Bands. Its upper limit range is not fixed and changes with the rolling of stock prices. When the stock price increases, the band becomes wider. When the amplitude of rise and fall decreases, the band becomes narrower. BOLL index has become a popular index widely used in the market due to its flexibility, intuition and trend.

## MACD Index

Smooth Similarities and Differences Moving Average (MACD) is derived from the double moving average and calculated by subtracting the slow-moving average from the fast-moving average. MACD is easier and faster to read than simply analyzing the difference between double moving averages.

MACD consists of positive and negative difference (DIFF) and the average difference (DEA).

(1) Positive and Negative Difference (Diff). DIFF is the difference between fast and slow. The difference between fast and slow is that the parameters used in exponential smoothing are different. The short-term moving average is fast and the long-term moving average is slow.

(2) Average of Similarities and Differences (DEA). DEA is the moving average of DIFF, that is, the arithmetic average of continuous DIFF.

When DIFF breaks through DEA upward, it is a buy signal.

- When DIFF falls below DEA, it can only be considered as a return to the previous position and a profit.
- When DIFF and DEA are both positive, they belong to the multi-head market.

- When DIFF and DEA are both negative, they are short markets.

- When DIFF breaks through DEA downward, it is a sell signal.

- When DIFF breaks through DEA upwards, it can only be considered as a rebound.

On the graph drawn, DIFF and DEA form two fast- and slow-moving average lines, and the buy and sell signals are determined by the intersection of these two lines. Obviously, the MACD index of Zhou K-line has high accuracy in judging the turning point of medium and long lines, which can be used as the preferred reference index for medium and long line investors.

Stock index futures provide a two-way trading mechanism, which can provide the market with hedging balance power, change the sharp rise and fall brought about by unilateral markets, help to form the internal stability mechanism of the stock market and cultivate a mature team of institutional investors. The biggest characteristics of GEM are low threshold entry and strict operation, and these factors can help enterprises gain financing opportunities, which is true for both small and medium businesses.

## Stock Index Futures

Stock Index Futures (STOCK INDEX FUTURES) is the full name of stock index futures. It is a financial futures contract with stock index as its subject matter. Both parties have agreed to buy and sell the target index at a certain date in the future according to the size of the stock index determined in advance.

### Characteristics of Stock Index Futures

Stock index futures and ordinary commodity futures have basically no essential difference except when they are due for delivery.

### Functions of Stock Index Futures

Since the 1970s, the volatility of stock markets in western countries has become increasingly intense, and investors' demand to avoid systemic risks in the stock market has become more and more urgent. The risks in the stock market can be divided into two parts: non-systematic risks and systematic risks. Non-systematic risks can usually be reduced through decentralized investment, while systematic risks are difficult to avoid through decentralized investment.

People began to try to transform the stock index into a tradable futures contract, and use it to hedge all stocks to avoid systemic risks, so stock index futures came into being with its function.

For example, investors who are worried about the decline of the stock market can hedge the systematic risk of the overall decline of the stock market by selling future contracts on their stock index. This is beneficial to alleviating the impact of collective selling on the stock market. The utilization of stock index futures may also help state-owned enterprises to raise funds directly in the securities market. In addition, stock index futures can cause the impact of fund cashing on the market to dawdle.

## How Are Stocks and Stock Index Futures Different From Each Other?

Both the stocks and stock index futures are traded on exchanges. In domestic market, the Financial Futures Exchange is in charge of stock index futures exchanges, where the shares are listed on the Stock Exchange and New York Stock Exchange. The two are different financial instruments and are quite different.

In addition, stock index futures have important advantages, such as providing more convenient short selling, lower transaction cost, higher leverage ratio, and higher market liquidity.

It is reported that in the UK, for a futures trading account with an initial margin of only 2,500 pounds, it can trade up to 70,000 pounds in 100 index futures of the Financial Times, with a leverage ratio of 28: 1. Since the amount of margin paid is determined according to the index futures' value in the market, the exchange will decide whether to add margin or whether to withdraw the excess amount. The price, of course, is determined by the market.

Also a kind of futures trading, the stock index futures has common features with commodity futures in operation mechanism and risk management, such as the same use of margin system, leverage amplification effect, daily non-debt settlement, etc. Stock index futures and commodity futures look the same, but there are also many differences.

In the secondary stock market, the role of stock index futures will critically modify its trading pattern. It will also strengthen the characteristics of the game between market institutions. With the gradual recognition of private equity funds by the state and the liberalization of policies, the financial management plan for private equity fund accounts will surely become the mainstream of the stock index futures market.

## Trading Process of Stock Index Futures

Before trading stock index futures, investors must have a clear understanding and understanding of each link of the transaction to avoid risks caused by the unfamiliar rules. The whole trading process of stock index futures can be divided into four steps: account opening, trading, settlement and delivery.

On the whole, stock index futures mainly bring three trading modes to investors: speculation, hedging and arbitrage. The main groups involved in the three models are different. Generally speaking, those who directly buy and sell stock index futures for speculative trading are mainly some individual investors with strong risk tolerance and pursuing high risks and high returns and some private equity funds. They are also active in the market, while institutional investors mostly use hedging and arbitrage trading.

## Stock Index Futures and Its Key Investment Points

The stock index futures have appealed to a variety of investors, as a lucrative investment tool. Under normal circumstances, investors should not use more than one-third of the total funds to engage in futures trading, and it is better not to use more than half of the total funds when holding a larger amount. According to this calculation, even if only one-hand stock index futures transaction is carried out, the minimum amount of capital required will exceed 100,000 dollars.

When calculating the amount of capital required by the stock index futures exchange, in addition to considering the minimum margin required by the futures company, a temporarily unused fund will be set aside to meet the requirements for additional margin that may arise. Therefore, considering the risk characteristics of stock index futures and investors' bearing capacity, it is suggested that individual investors with less than 500,000 available funds should not participate in the trading of stock index futures.

In general, stock market judgment methods can be divided into technical analysis and fundamental analysis. Among them, stock technical analysis is still applicable to future stock index futures, but fundamental analysis is limited. In the fundamental analysis of stock index futures, international market and other factors should also be considered. In general, when investors enter the stock index futures market from stocks, they need to change not only the investment concept but also the thinking mode.

By this we have completed analysis topic in stock market. In the next chapter we will discuss about risks that stock market comes with. Let us dive into them in detail. As a stock investor one should be always get ready to cope with losses as it is part of the game. But there are only few successful investors that take security measures to minimize the loss. We will in the next chapter look at a bunch of strategies that will help us understand things in a better way about risks and how to face them.

# CHAPTER 7

# Risks in Stock Market

As the saying goes, "The stock market is risky, so be careful when entering the market." Everyone knows that the stock market is a high-risk place, but in recent years, stock market has entered a period of rapid development. Understanding risks and traps and mastering how to prevent them are of great help to investors.

There are risks in the stock market and caution should be exercised when entering the market.

Stock market risk usually refers to the risk that investors will not be able to make profits or even recover their costs after entering the stock market. It is mainly reflected in the fact that after investors buy a stock at a certain price and when the stock price drops sharply as a result, they cannot sell the stock at a lower price than when they bought resulting in a hold-up phenomenon.

What are the risks in the stock market? How to recognize and prevent it?

## What is Stock Market Risk?

Risk refers to the possibility of loss or damage. Judging from the definition of risk, there are mainly two kinds of stock investment risks: one is the possible loss of investors' income and principal; The other is the possible loss of investors' income and purchasing power of principal.

Stock investment risk has obvious duality, that is, its existence is objective, absolute, subjective and relative. It is both inevitable and controllable. Investors' control of stock risks is to minimize the risk-bearing cost by using a series of investment strategies and technical means according to the duality of risks.

## Types of Stock Market Risks

As the saying goes, "success also means stock, failure also means stock", which directly reflects the characteristics of high risks and high returns of stock. In order to avoid risks and gain profits as much as possible, investors need to understand various common stock market risks.

People often say that in the stock market, ordinary people's intuition sometimes surpasses the theories of experts. The founder of Adam's theory which is still Valid, after years of enthusiastic research on technical analysis, finally rejected all his research results because he believed that the trend in the stock market could not be predicted. All analysis tools had inevitable defects. Any analysis tool could not predict the trend of the stock market absolutely and accurately.

All the data and charts in the technical analysis only represent the past and reflect the information of the past. It is only possible to predict the future with a certain probability. Compared with the unpredictable stock market, nothing is impossible. For technical analysis, shareholders should look at it dialectically, combine the results of technical analysis with actual trends, and follow the trend to avoid risks as much as possible.

## How to Prevent Stock Market Risks?

The existence of risks and traps cannot be changed, but investors can apply relevant experience and knowledge to avoid risks and prevent traps as much as possible.

### 1. Master the professional knowledge of securities

In order to avoid risks and gain profits from investments, new investors must do the following two things before trading stocks.

(1) To understand the risks and traps of the stock market, one must know and understand the

corresponding stock knowledge in detail.

(2) According to certain professional knowledge, analyze and avoid these risks and traps.

## 2. Avoid mistakes in stock market operation

Although many ordinary investors are cautious and cautious after entering the market, there are still a lot of assets that are lost as the index rises and falls. This is mainly because many investors have big or small mistakes in actual operations. Let's look at what common mistakes investors have in the stock market.

(1) There is no stop loss concept.

The setting of stop-loss and stop-gain is very important. Many investors always fantasize about buying at the lowest point and selling at the highest point. They don't know the stock market clearly. They must stop-loss when breaking the position.

(2) Buy only cheap stocks.

It is necessary to know that the low price of the stock price is only compared with the previous period. If the upside is too heavy, the momentum of the stock rise is not enough to cross the resistance zone, and the stock price is also difficult to rise. Buying such stocks blindly only on the basis of the low price will bring great losses to investors.

(3) like to predict the market.

Many investors like to "predict" stock prices through technical analysis. In fact, for technical analysis, investors should look at it dialectically, combine the results of technical analysis with actual trends, and follow the trend to avoid risks as much as possible.

(4) When the quilt cover is worn, it will be sold after it is removed.

Technically, it is not advisable to wait for the deep-seated stocks to be unwound. Investors cannot passively wait for the results. Active measures are the right path.

(5) Tracking the purchase of active stock.

Usually you need to buy in a short time of 15 minutes before and after the rise in active stock. When ordinary investors find active stock, they often miss the best buying opportunity.

## 3. Analyze the environment and seize the opportunity.

As the saying goes, "when choosing stocks is not as good as when choosing them", choosing a good investment timing can reduce the possibility of the selected stocks falling and effectively avoid systemic risks. To grasp the general investment opportunity, investors can pay attention to the following two details.

(1) Political changes.

Political factors can easily affect social stability. If regime change brings social unrest, the stock market will fall.

(2) Price rise.

Under normal circumstances, after the price rises, the stock price of the corresponding type generally rises and Prices fell and the corresponding share price fell.

Investors should pay due attention to such large environments as political events, inflation and price changes, cultivate enthusiasm for state affairs and international current affairs, understand the current situation and trend of national policy implementation and economic development. They should also have a keen judgment on the possible impact of macroeconomic changes on the economic situation.

## 4. Choose the right investment method

After all, the stock market is a high-risk place. Even if you adopt more skills and learn more theories, you will inevitably encounter risks. Choosing the right investment method can effectively avoid various risks in the stock market.

(1) adopt diversified investment methods.

Using different investment methods for different stocks according to their characteristics can achieve the purpose of dispersing risks through diversified investment methods. Investors should not only adopt a single investment mode, but also combine long-term, medium-term and short-term investment modes.

(2) Diversify investment and reserve enough spare funds.

The purpose of diversification is to diversify risks, reduce risks and avoid risks. Its method is to combine different securities into investment portfolios. Of course, the risk is not the more dispersed the better, but should be enough. Retail investors with small principal should be relatively concentrated, which is relatively low in cost and easy to form economies of scale.

## 5. Formulate a reasonable investment plan

In fact, when many investors buy stocks, they usually buy a lot of stocks randomly and buy a variety of different stocks in their own accounts, but the result is often to buy a large number of loss-making stocks. In view of the different age, occupation, income and economic conditions of each investor, each investor should have his own unique investment plan.

(1) according to their own investment ability to choose an investment strategy.

(2) Determine the investment scale according to its own financial resources.

(3) Determine the investment cycle according to the available time and funds.

(4) Decide the investment direction and choose the investment object according to their tolerance to risks.

(5) Make investment plans according to the energy of investors.

## 6. Be vigilant against unhealthy advisory bodies.

Most stock investors across the country are losing money, while consulting firms are pocketing large amounts of money easily. The mystery is difficult for outsiders to see.

Most of the stock consulting agencies are following the operation mode of "not speculating in stocks but speculating in stocks". They believe that if everyone believes that there is gold on the mountain across the river, you should not go for gold, but run boats on the river. Therefore, this once again reminds investors that stocks should still believe in themselves and cannot easily believe any gossip!

## 7. Pay Attention to Safety in Online Stock Trading

With the development of the Internet and the popularization of computers, more and more people are surfing the Internet, and online stock trading has gradually become a trend. Online trading has many advantages and is easy to operate and is not subject to geographical restrictions. However, when conducting online trading, it is also necessary to pay attention to its safety.

(1) Protect the transaction password. Change the password frequently to ensure that it is not known by others. In addition, when using the Internet to conduct transactions, do not easily download unknown software, so as not to provide opportunities for computer hackers.

(2) The operation process should be cautious. When online trading fails, you can Inquire about the market price or issue trading instructions by phone to avoid unnecessary losses caused by untimely operation.

(3) withdraw from the trading system. After the transaction is completed, the account must be withdrawn correctly and the transaction system must be shut down, so as not to leave any chance for those who are plotting against the law.

## Prevent various traps in the stock market

The difference between traps and risks is that traps are artificially created by improper means, with the purpose of deliberately inducing investors to enter and seek benefits from them.

This section mainly introduces common traps in the stock market.

False trading is one of the acts of manipulating the market. There are four specific types.

(1) Pretending to buy and sell:

including quoting the price in vain, not making any actual transaction, and being both the buyer and the seller. Or it may be agreed in advance that Party A will sell it to Party B, and then Party B will return it at the original price, but the ownership of the securities will not be transferred.

(2) Conspiracy to Buy and Sell:

That is, Party A and Party B buy and sell at the agreed price, repeatedly hype up the stock price, and then sell at a really high price to make a profit.

(3) Entrustment or entrustment of fake trading and collusive trading:

The entrusting party and the entrusted party are used to conduct fake trading and collusive trading to control the stock price.

**(4) False promotion:**

repeatedly buying or selling certain securities in a row to show the active trading of such stocks, to create momentum for the wind to rise, and to induce others to fall for it.

For example, in October 1994, the business department of Development Centre, a securities company, continuously traded A shares on a buy-and-sell basis, resulting in a 157% increase in the closing price on that day over the previous day. The Development Centre Business Department of the securities company sold shares the next day, earning 2.38 million.

The trap of stock evaluation refers to the fact that some stock evaluators are obsessed with profits and mistakenly guide stock investors in order to achieve a certain purpose. Therefore, shareholders should also be careful when listening to them. They cannot fully believe them and always pay attention to themselves as the decision makers. Stock analysts only provide reference opinions and will not be held responsible for the losses of shareholders.

Stock evaluation is a kind of analysis activity carried out by more senior people in the stock industry, which covers TV, magazines, newspapers and various financial media. As investors do not all have research on stocks, and there are many knowledge and data to be analyzed, stock evaluation by professionals is a guideline for many investors to buy and sell stocks. In this regard, shareholders should pay attention to the following contents.

(1) As stock evaluation experts have a certain influence among shareholders, dealers and listed companies will try every means to cooperate with some so-called experts to set up a fraud through their stock evaluation to induce investors to operate according to their ideas and finally achieve the goal of illegal profits. This kind of stock evaluation news is the most harmful. Investors must be cautious about stock evaluation news and insist on independent thinking.

(2) The factors affecting the stock market are complex and changeable, and the risk of the stock market itself is unpredictable. Any stock evaluation expert's prediction of the stock market is only based on the possibility of some theoretical analysis, and cannot accurately predict the trend of the stock market. It is also inevitable that there will be wrong judgment. However, if the wrong judgment is adopted by shareholders, serious losses will be caused.

Investors should treat concepts and stock reviews in books prudently and objectively. They should not blindly follow, superstition famous sayings of famous experts, or follow others' opinions. They should learn to use reverse thinking because most people are always wrong, and only a few people will master the truth.

Large investors use investors' psychology of superstitious technology to analyze data and charts, deliberately pulling up and suppressing stock indexes, causing technical charts to form a certain line shape and making luring investors to buy or sell in large quantities, thus achieving their goal of making a fortune. The line type of technical chart caused by such fraudulence is called fraudulent line.

During the distribution of the main force, in order to make the withdrawal process more smooth, various means are often used to attract the followers, so as to get out of the way. The following are the tricks commonly used when distributing the main force.

(1) False Breakthrough of Cheating Line.

The main force creates an upward breakthrough in the pattern of finishing, even the illusion of an increase in price, but this breakthrough is a false breakthrough, especially in the relative top stage, with the aim of attracting investors to follow suit.

Usually this strength does not last long, but tends to rise and fall after a few days, and at the same time releases huge turnover, which means the start of diving. If investors encounter this kind of situation, they should be judged as false breakthroughs and should leave in time.

(2) The closing price cheats the line.

The closing price refers to the closing price of a stock before the end of the day's trading activity on the stock exchange.

For example, retail investors saw that a stock had been going low one day, but it suddenly soared in late trading, making the K-line chart look very attractive to attract the following trend. This is usually the banker to confuse short-term customers with small profits, while taking the opportunity to escape in the oscillation.

(3) pull tail city cheat line.

Some main players did not make any moves during the whole trading day, but often within a few minutes near the closing price, the main players pushed up the stock price rapidly with several large orders in a row. We call this kind of pull-up as a kind of pull-up that encourages growth. Generally speaking, this kind of pull-up often occurs for several days in a row, the purpose of which is to make the closing price, thus creating a perfect technical figure on the daily chart.

Most stock investors mainly analyze and judge the buying and selling timing of stocks through K-line and other technical analysis indicators. As a result, many stock market manipulators manipulate the stock price and trading volume to make some false buying and selling timing patterns appear in the technical analysis chart, which is commonly referred to as fraudulent lines. The emergence of fraudulent lines warned investors not to rely too much on technical analysis indicators, otherwise they would easily be cheated.

In short, in the stock market, it is the technical figure that changes with the change of the stock price, not the stock price that changes with the change of the technical figure. All technical figures can only be used for reference, and technical analysis should be combined with fundamental analysis and the general situation of the stock market when making decisions, instead of relying solely on technical analysis.

Rat Trading is a kind of "food price" practice in which unscrupulous brokers are unfaithful to customers. Specifically, the banker uses his own funds to build a low-level position before using public funds to raise the stock price. After using public funds to raise the stock price to a high level, the individual position takes the lead in selling for profit.

The reason is that after the securities firms pulled up the stocks, a large number of rat warehouses buried at the bottom poured out and the securities firms took orders at high positions. The result is that the securities firms have suffered heavy losses and the rat storehouse has made a lot of money. This is the main form of securities firms being hollowed out today.

The K-line pattern of "rat storehouse" generally appears when the stock price is about to rise, and the stock price will show a good trend in a period of time after the K-line is formed. The technical characteristics of rat storehouse are shown

### Insider trading

Insider trading refers to the act of obtaining the company's insider information that has an impact on the stock price through improper means before the company discloses the internal information, and using the information to conduct stock trading, or the act of divulging the insider information and making suggestions to others for buying and selling stocks. The essence of insider trading is to use unfair competition means to gain profits, which violates the principle of "openness, fairness and justice" in the securities market and also violates relevant laws and regulations.

Insider information objectively means that insiders use insider information to buy or sell securities, or suggest others to buy or sell securities according to insider information. Insiders divulge inside information to others so that others can use the information for insider trading. Non-insiders obtain insider information through improper means or other means, and suggest others to buy or sell stocks after buying or selling according to the information. Insider information mainly includes the following contents.

- Securities issuers have entered into important contracts that may have significant impacts.

- The fact that shareholders holding more than 5% of the issuer's ordinary shares issued abroad have increased or decreased by more than 2% of the total amount of the shares issued abroad.

- Changes in national policies that may have a significant impact on stock market prices.

- The issuer fails to repay the due major debts and other defaults.

- Significant changes have taken place in the issuer's production and operation environment.

- The issuer shall pay dividends, increase capital and expand shares.

- The issuer enters bankruptcy and liquidation.

- The issuer incurred significant debts.

- Significant changes have taken place in the issuer's business policies or business scope.

- The issuer commits major investment or purchases large amount of long-term assets.

- The issuer incurred significant operating or non-operating losses.

- Acquisition or merger, division, etc. of the issuer.

- The issuer's assets suffered heavy losses.

- The chairman of the board of directors, more than 30% of directors or general manager of the issuer have changed.

By this we have completed our stock market investing course in brief. This book has learnt a lot of things to you about investing in detail. You need to further improve your knowledge by watching trading tutorials or a series. There are also different options like forex trading, foreign exchanges that can be learnt in detail. Learn them to improve your knowledge.

# CONCLUSION

Thank you for making it through to the end of Stock Market Investing for Beginners, let's hope it was informative and able to provide you with all of the tools you need to achieve your goals whatever they may be.

The next step is to use this knowledge to develop your skills and implement them in trading. Trading needs a great psychological power because if you are unable to cope up with the losses you may entail you will give up. Sheer positivity and hope can make investors and traders succeed in very less time.

You can use different strategies to use your capital investment. It may take you some time to get settled in the arena. But when you get a hand on it there is nothing that can stop you. Now try to look at different stocks available in the market using any web app or mobile and try to analyze using real time stock data. All the best for your trading career and always believes in optimism.

Finally, if you found this book useful in any way, a review on Amazon is always appreciated!

www.ingramcontent.com/pod-product-compliance
Lightning Source LLC
Chambersburg PA
CBHW060847220526
45466CB00003B/1267